Black Diamonds

The Wisdom of Booker T. Washington
Originally titled
BLACK-BELT DIAMONDS
Gems from the Speeches, Addresses
and Talks to Students

of

BOOKER T. WASHINGTON
Principal of Tuskegee Institute, Tuskegee, Ala.

Selected and Arranged by
VICTORIA EARLE MATTHEWS
Author of *Aunt Lindy*, etc.

Introduction by
T. THOMAS FORTUNE

Health Communications, Inc.
Deerfield Beach, Florida

© 1898 Victoria Earle Matthews, 1990 Mnemosyne Publishing Co., Inc.,
1995 Frank Wills
ISBN 1-55874-343-X

Publisher: Health Communications, Inc.
            3201 S.W. 15th Street
            Deerfield Beach, Florida 33442-81190

Introduction

♦

A French philosopher has said that "the romances of fact are stranger than the romances of fiction." A close study of the lives of successful men in all periods of the world's history will show this to be true. And history is simply the record of human effort, of the success of individuals who have done the thinking and the acting, who have made a pathway for mankind from barbarism to civilization. No imagination can conceive a character in which the romantic element can be compared with that to be found in the life of every man who has been conspicuous in the world's thought and effort. The most successful poets and novelists have drawn upon the great storehouse of history for materials for their most successful and lasting work. All else has perished, or is perishing. And this will continue to be so while success and failure shall remain the basis of the heroic and the pathetic in human life.

Strangely enough, the Southern States have produced only two men, since the War of the Rebellion, who have achieved a national reputation. These two men are Henry W. Grady, of Georgia, and Booker T. Washington, of Alabama. The one represented the white South, with which he was identified by blood and sympathy, and spoke for it alone, and secured for himself an audience as wide as the continent, which has become—in what it stands for rather than in what it is—the hope and inspiration of the oppressed and downtrodden of all lands; and he was dangerous because he spoke for a part and not for the whole of the Southern people, because he contended for a part and not for the whole truth, as it is related to manhood and citizenship, and to that Christian charity which embraces all the children of men. The other represents the whole South, because he is identified with the whole South by blood and sympathy, and he speaks for the whole South, and has secured for himself an audience as wide as the continent; and he is a safe and a helpful man because he speaks for the whole Southern people, because he contends for the whole and not for a part of the truth, as it is related to manhood and citizenship, and to that Christian charity which embraces all the children of men.

Mr. Grady laid it down as the corner-stone of his faith, and was content to rest his fame with posterity upon it, that "the supremacy of the white race of the South must be maintained forever, and the domination of the Negro race resisted at all points and at all hazards, because the white race is the superior race. This is the declaration of no new truth; it has abided forever in the marrow of our bones, and shall run forever with the blood that feeds Anglo-Saxon hearts."

This sentiment is opposed to Christian philosophy, and is specifically disavowed by the Federal Constitution, which does not recognize the divine right of the Anglo-Saxon race or the Afro-American race, or any other race comprehended in our American citizenship; and the life was shot out of it on a hundred battlefields in the War of the Rebellion!

Mr. Washington said (in his address at the Alumni Dinner of Harvard University, June 24, 1896, after having received the honorary degree of Master of Arts), and he is content to rest his fame with posterity upon it, that "while we are thus being tested, I beg of you to remember that wherever our life touches yours we help or we hinder. Wherever your life touches ours you make us stronger or weaker. No member of your race in any part of the country can harm the meanest member of mine without the proudest and bluest blood in Massachusetts being degraded. When Mississippi commits crime, New England commits crime, and in so much lowers the standard of your civilization. There is no escape—man drags man down, or man lifts man up.

"In working out our destiny, while the main burden and centre of activity must be with us, we shall need in a large measure, in the years that are to come, as we have had in the past, the help, the encouragement, the guidance that the strong can give the weak. Thus helped, we of both races in the South soon shall throw off the shackles of racial and sectional prejudices, and rise, as Harvard University has risen, and as we all should rise, above the clouds of ignorance, narrowness, and selfishness, into that atmosphere, that pure sunshine, where it will be our highest ambition to serve man, our brother, regardless of race or past condition."

Upon another occasion, Mr. Washington said: "I thank God I have grown to the point where I can sympathize with a white man as much as I can with a black man, where I can sympathize with a Southern white man as much as I can with a Northern white man." Again: "The black man who cannot let love and sympathy go out to a white man is but half free."

The difference between Mr. Grady and Mr. Washington is to be found in the fact that the one was an Anglo-Saxon American, and the other an Afro-American; that the one was born a free man, and the other a slave; that the one was educated to believe God made freedom and opportunity for His white children alone, the other that He made them for all His children—of Ham and Shem and Japheth, the black and white and yellow. And so each, according to his lights, builded—the one upon sand, the other upon rock, the one for the present, the other for posterity!

These two men were born orators of great power. The one spent his genius and energy in seeking to clinch the rivets in the chain that bound the intellect and the soul of two races—"one as to the hand, separate as to the fingers"—to the blighting prejudices and dogmas of the dead past, to the decaying carcass of slavery; while the other spends his genius and energy in seeking to loosen the rivets in the chain of the dead past, to unite the whole people for mutual help and sympathy, to make the freedom of both races a positive force for power and for good in our national life—to heal up the wounds of the past, that we may be strong as a united people to enjoy to the fullest extent the destiny which God, in His mercy, has set as a prize for our high calling among the nations of the earth—and the people of the North and the South and the West, lend willing ears to the "tidings of great joy" which it is his privilege to deliver.

And these two men were born educators. The one planted a newspaper, which grew and waxed strong, so that it became as an oracle, speaking as with authority, and it will bear upon its front the impress of his genius and of his limitations—of his provincialism in the matters of race and of country—and remain a disturbing element, because out of joint with the irresistible philosophy of human and national progress, for many years to come; while the other planted an institution of learning in a rich soil[1], which has

---

[1] The Tuskegee Normal and Industrial Institute was founded at Tuskegee, Alabama, in a church made of logs, by Mr. Washington, seventeen years ago. It has steadily grown in extent and importance, so that today it contains nearly one thousand pupils and about one hundred instructors and helpers, and is conducted at an annual outlay of something

been and is and will remain a nursery of Christian love and charity for all the children of men, and of a patriotism as broad and deep as our Declaration of Independence, the strongest pronouncement of human freedom ever made, and as abiding as the Federal Constitution, upon which our institutions rest "in the love of man and the fear of God."

The voice of Henry W. Grady is silent in death. While he lived, "the proud scion of a proud race" divided the honors, as the South's representative orator and educator, with Booker T. Washington, the humble offspring of a slave woman who could not call her soul her own. Fate could go no further in giving vitality and force to the poet's declaration, that "one touch of Nature makes the whole world kin," and in teaching the sublime lesson that—

> Honor and worth from no condition rise;
> Act well your part—there all the honor lies.

Mr. Washington still lives; and today the South possesses no voice stronger than his—that has the nation for

---

like a hundred thousand dollars, all of which is raised by voluntary subscriptions, except about five thousand dollars per annum contributed by the State of Alabama. It also receives assistance from the Slater and Peabody Funds, whose active agent, the Hon. J. L. M. Curry, is a strong friend of the Tuskegee Institute work. But too much of Mr. Washington's time and energy is devoted to the work of securing the funds necessary to keep the Institute going. An ample endowment is imperatively needed. Mr. Washington's idea of education was imbibed from General S.C. Armstrong, who founded the Hampton Institute, in 1868. It is thoroughly normal and industrial in character. The dignity of labor is the cornerstone of the whole structure.

an audience when he uses it, that is teaching Christian love and sympathy and national unity with like power and success. The God that lifted him out of bondage has made him a great power for good in the land. And it is due to the Southern people—to all the Southern people—to say that they recognize the native ability and the consecration to service—the sustaining the weak, and the lifting up of the fallen—of the man, the tower of strength, who has taken the place so long and worthily filled by Frederick Douglass, as "the guide, philosopher, and friend" of the ten million Afro-American citizens of the Republic, with whom his lot is more particularly cast, and to emphasize the fact that one of the strongest elements of his strength and influence is the respect and confidence of the whole Southern people which he enjoys in such unstinted measure; a respect and confidence which, added to that of the people of the North and West, have enabled him to erect and sustain a light-house of knowledge in the Black Belt of Alabama, whose reflection, whose pervasive influence, is blinding the eyes of ignorance and prejudice, so that men may see the beauty and the wealth that abound in Nature, and thus intelligently lay hold upon them for their use and comfort, and that they may see and imbibe that reverence for the Creator and love of mankind in which the happiness of the people and the strength of the nation abide.

It is appropriate to say this much, in submitting to the reader the collection of some of the wise thoughts which Mr. Washington has uttered at various times and places, and which have been culled, with so much of industry and discrimination and devotion to the life-work of the man, by Mrs. Matthews.

T. THOMAS FORTUNE
1898

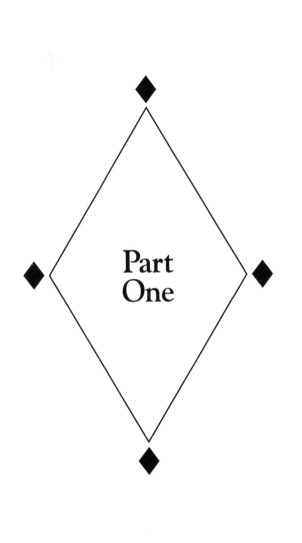

Part
One

Heart of the Race

General Armstrong—he was the heart of the race; his great heart held us all so constantly, so strongly, so tenderly, that it gave way at a time when most men begin to live.

Memorial to General Armstrong

He Must Be Counted

One third of the population of the South is of the Negro race. No enterprise seeking the material, civil, or moral welfare of this section can disregard this element of our population and reach the highest success.

Atlanta Speech

The Negro's Mission

I think a part of his [the Negro's] mission is going to be to teach white men a lesson of patience, forbearance, and forgiveness. I think he is going to show the people of this country what it is possible for a race to achieve when starting under adverse conditions. Again, I believe he is destined to preach a lesson of supreme trust in God and loyalty to his country, even when his country has not been at all times loyal to him. I think my people will excel in the missionary spirit. It will take the form of reaching down after the less fortunate both at home and abroad.

Our Day

◆

The Negro's Home

The Negro has a genuine interest in this country—in the South. It is his home, and he is going to remain in the South. He is not here to grab a few dollars and then return to some foreign shore.

Southern States Farm Magazine

◆

"We Claim Him"

It takes one hundred percent of Caucasian blood to make a white American. The minute it is proven that a man possesses one one-hundredth part of Negro blood in his veins, it makes him a black man. He falls to our side; we claim him. The ninety-nine percent of white blood counts for nothing when weighed against one percent of Negro blood.

Development of the Negro

Obeying the Scriptures

If ever there was a people that have obeyed the Scriptural injunction, "If they smite thee on one cheek, turn the other also," that people has been the American Negro.

Man Our Brother

◆

Self-Respect

Self-Respect will bring the Negro many rights now denied him.

Negro Conference

◆

Loyalty

Whether in slavery or in freedom, we have always been loyal to the stars and stripes.

Democracy and Education

◆

The Negro Originally Honest

The Negro in his original native state was an honest race; it was slavery that unmanned him in this respect.

Twentieth Century Club (New York)

Basis of Prejudice

The prejudice against the Negro is not on account of color, but because of the badge of slavery—the slavery we used to be in and the industrial slavery we are now in.

Industrial Freedom

◆

Talk Versus Action

It is all very well to bewail our wrongs. I feel them as keenly as anyone else. But, I think, we have had quite enough talk about them, and that the thing to do now is to try to get our rights.

Duty of the Hour

◆

Power of Faith

You have all, doubtless, read that portion of the Bible which tells of the woman who touched the hem of Christ's garment, and thereby showed her faith. That in itself was a little thing; and yet this power of human confidence is something that we do not always realize. We do not always appreciate its significance. How often do we come in contact with men and women in whose presence we may dwell only for

a short time, but we can never look on their counte-
nances or be in any way associated with them without
being made better, or lifted up, as it were.

Sunday Evening Tuskegee Talks

◆

Mutual Dependence

Wherever our life touches yours we help or we hinder.

Negro's Future in America

◆

Education the Only Hope

Education is the sole and only hope of the Negro race
in America. Transportation, colonization, and other
schemes of misguided enthusiasts, are impracticable
and futile.

The Negro's Hope

◆

His Recompense

If the Negro who has been oppressed and denied rights
in a Christian land can help you, North and South, to
rise, can be a medium of your rising into the atmosphere of generous brotherhood and self-forgetfulness,

he will see in it a recompense for all that he has suffered in the past.

Home Missionary Meeting (New York)

◆

Ignorance Against Intelligence

Can you make your intelligence affect us in the same ratio that our ignorance affects you?

Democracy and Education

◆

Eagerness for Knowledge

No schoolhouse has been opened for us that has not been filled.

Negro's Future in America

◆

A New Race

We are a new race, as it were, and the time, attention, and activity of any race are taken up during the first fifty or one hundred years in getting a start.

Sunday Evening Tuskegee Talks

"One Touch of Nature"

We are led into saying that there is no difference between us and other people. We must admit that there is a difference produced by the unequal opportunities. To argue otherwise is to discredit the effects of slavery.

Stumbling Blocks

Ballot-Box and Schoolhouse

I beg of you, further, that, in the degree that you close the ballot-box against the ignorant, you open the schoolhouse.

Constitutional Convention (Louisiana)

What the Negro Needs

What are the cardinal needs among the seven millions of colored people in the South, most of whom are to be found on the plantations? Roughly, these needs may be stated as food, clothing, shelter, education, proper habits, and a settlement of race relations.

Awakening of the Negro

Responsibility for Slavery

The time has come, it seems to me, for Northern men, Southern men, black men and white men, to blot out their prejudices and look matters squarely in the face as they are. The whole country was responsible for slavery.

The South and Lynch-Law

◆

An Equal Chance

I only ask an equal chance in the world for the Negro.

The Negro's Way to Liberty

◆

Phillips Brooks

There are persons whose lives are so much like that of Christ's, who have so much genuine Christianity in them, that we cannot come in contact with them, we cannot even steal a glance at their faces, without being made stronger and better. It is said that on one cold, wintry day, when snow and rain were falling, and the day was one to make a person despondent, Phillips Brooks was walking through the streets of Boston. At once those who saw him and looked upon his countenance saw a ray of sunshine. Why? Because that man was so full of the "milk of human kindness," so overflowing with love for humanity, that no man, however degraded and besotted a specimen of humanity he was, could look upon that face without being helped, without feeling that he, with every other human being, had a place in the heart of great Phillips Brooks.

Sunday Evening Tuskegee Talks

Dishonest Voting

Study the history of the South, and you will find that where there has been most dishonesty in voting there you will find the lowest moral condition of both races.

Constitutional Convention (Louisiana)

♦

The Good Samaritans

Religion should be a thing of every-day living—less Levi, more Good Samaritan.

Negro Conference

Only Two Alternatives

To the rank and file of our aspiring youth, seeking an opening in life, to me but two alternatives present themselves, as matters now stand—to live a menial in the North, or a semi-free man in the South. This brings us face to face with Northern competition and Southern prejudice, and between them I have no hesitancy in saying that the Negro can find his way to the front sooner through Southern prejudice than through Northern competition. The one decreases; the other increases.

Lincoln University

Pagans No Longer

We went into slavery in this country pagans; we came out Christians.

Our New Citizen

"Cast Down Your Bucket"

To those of my race who depend upon bettering their condition in a foreign land, or who underestimate the importance of cultivating friendly relations with the Southern white man who is their next-door neighbor, I would say: "Cast down your bucket where you are.

Cast it down in making friends, in every honorable way, of the people of all races by whom you are surrounded. Cast it down in agriculture, mechanics, in commerce, in domestic service, and in the professions."

Atlanta Speech

◆

All Fools Alike

A fool in Africa is not better than a fool in America.

Negro Conference

◆

Business Opportunity

The Negro's present great opportunity in the South is in the matter of business; and success in the South is going to constitute the foundation for success and relief along other lines.

The Negro's Opportunity

◆

Our Mother Tongue

We went into slavery without a language; we came out speaking the proud Anglo-Saxon tongue.

Our New Citizen

Equality of Opportunity

Let the young colored man feel that he can be not only waiter in hotels but part proprietor, that on Pullman cars he can be not only porter but conductor, and he will go forward.

The Negro's Way to Liberty

◆

The South as the Field

It is in the South that the Negro is given a man's chance in the commercial world.

Hamilton Club (Chicago)

◆

Advice to White Men

To those of the white race who look to the incoming of those of foreign birth and strange tongue and habits for the prosperity of the South, I would repeat what I say to my own race, "Cast down your bucket where you are. Cast it down among the eight million Negroes, whose habits you know, whose fidelity you have tested in days when to have proved treacherous meant the ruin of your firesides."

Atlanta Speech

He Learned to Labor

If in the providence of God the Negro got any good out of slavery, he got the habit of work.

Carnegie Hall (New York)

New Industrial Era

The South is about to enter an era of industrial development that will be almost without a parallel.

Our New Citizen

What Education Does

We teach the Negro that labor is not degrading. This education multiplies his wants, and we try to keep pace with his widening desires by giving him the skill to satisfy them.

The Rise of the Negro

♦

Fate of Laggards

We must catch the spirit of modern progress and achievement, or be shut out by those who have.

Education Meeting (Milwaukee)

Serious Mistakes

Immediately after freedom we made serious mistakes.
We began at the top. We made these mistakes, not
because we were black people, but because we were
ignorant and inexperienced.

Association Hall (Philadelphia)

◆

The One Drawback

The one great drawback to the development of the
South is the lack of skilled and educated labor.

Industrial Development

◆

Adaptability Needed

We must adjust ourselves to the changed conditions,
or be left behind in the march of progress.

Spirit of the Coming One

◆

Heritage of Slavery

Look at the vast wealth of undeveloped resources that
encompasses almost every Southern community—

look at the fertile fields or the worn lands still
in bondage to ignorant labor and the ante-bellum
agricultural system.

Industrial Growth

◆

What Law Cannot Do

The mere fiat of the law could not make a dependent
man independent; it could not make an ignorant
voter an intelligent voter, could not make one man
respect another man. These results come by beginning at the bottom, and working upwards, by recog-
nizing our weaknesses as well as our strength, by tan-
gible evidences of our worthiness to occupy the highest position.

The Emancipator

◆

Correct Education

We are training colored men to be self-supporting,
saving, and business-like.

The Rise of the Negro

The Shirker

Never get into a rut. You cannot afford to do a thing poorly. You are more injured in shirking your work or half-doing a job than the person for whom you are working.

Sunday Evening Tuskegee Talks

How Life Is Measured

Do not think life consists of dress and show. Remember that everyone's life is measured by the power that that individual has to make the world better—this is all life is.

Sunday Evening Tuskegee Talks

"What We Want"

What we want, and it is what America honors, is the man who can teach his followers how to overcome obstacles, how to find a way or make one.

Taking Advantage of Our Disadvantages

Trained Head and Hand

The hand, as well as the head, of every black boy and girl of the South should be trained to some useful occupation.

Age-Herald

♦

The Acceptable Thing

The acceptable thing is to do the most good in the shortest time at the least expense. It cannot be done by a single law, in a single day, with a single gift. Our school is a lever which has made of several hundred young men and women levers in their turn to lift up their race. The masses of colored people have got the habit of work, and only need a teacher, an object lesson.

In the Black Belt

♦

The Old Washerwoman

Without industrial education, when the black woman washes a shirt, she washes with both hands, both feet, and her whole body. An individual with industrial education will use a machine that washes ten times as many shirts in a given time with almost no expenditure of physical force; steam, electricity, or water doing the work.

Dedicatory Services (Avondale, Ohio)

◆

The Fate of the Pauper

No one cares for a man with empty head and pocket, no matter what his color is.

Sunday Evening Tuskegee Talks

◆

Where Profits Appear

We must not only teach the Negro to improve the methods of what are now classed as the lower forms of labor, but the Negro must be put in a position, by the use of intelligence and skill, to take his part in the higher forms of labor, up in the region where the profits appear.

Industrial Training

◆

What the World Desires

The world desires to know what a man can do, not what he knows.

Dignity of Labor

The Lyncher and the Lynched

Lynchings and burnings, which are often witnessed by numbers of young and tender children, do the race that inflicts these punishments, many times more harm, by blunting its moral sense, than the race or individual against whom they are directed.

The South and Lynch-Law

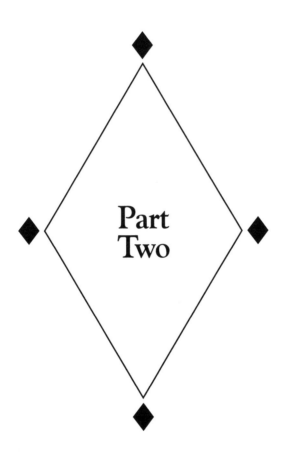

Part
Two

"Honesty the Best Policy"

That the Negro may be fitted for the fullest enjoyment of the privileges and responsibilities of our country, it is important that we be honest and candid with the Negro himself, whether our honesty and candor for the time being pleases him or displeases him.

Democracy and Education

◆

False Education

The young are not only educated without reference to the conditions of the age, but their minds are carefully and systematically trained in other directions. They see no triumph of intellect except in politics or the "learned" professions.

Progress

◆

Lack of Manufactories

There is hardly a county in the South that does not contain enough hard wood to manufacture all the wagons used in that county, and yet by far the larger proportion of wagons used in the South come from a distance. Even such simple things as ax-handles are often imported.

Industrial Education in the South

What a Thousand Dollars Will Do

Any colored man with a reasonable education, common sense, and business ability, can take a thousand dollars in cash and go into any Southern community and in five years be worth five thousand. He does not meet with the stern, relentless competition that he encounters when he butts up against a Northern Yankee.

The South as an Opening for a Business Career

◆

Generosity

Lay hold of something that will help you, and then use it to help somebody else.

Negro Conference

◆

The Slave of Duty

Show me a person who merely does as a duty what he is asked to do and I will show you a person who is never in constant demand—a person who is not going to be very valuable to humanity.

Sunday Evening Tuskegee Talks

Evil of Card-Playing

Do not play cards. Playing cards, you will insist, is no more harmful than playing dominoes or croquet; but it is a fact undeniable that playing cards leads to something more harmful than either of the games I have just mentioned. Card-playing has a history, and it is the experience of men who understand crime, who understand civilization in all its grades, that card-playing has been the source of any number of crimes. It leads to late hours, bad company, a betting proclivity, and, finally, it leads to the using of other people's money.

Sunday Evening Tuskegee Talks

♦

Moral Slavery

The slavery of ante-bellum times has passed away, but there is a moral slavery existing in the South which will take a long time to pass away.

Negroes and Mortgages

Dependence upon the North

In the great industrial awakening that is upon us, the skill to manage and operate our mills and factories, and convert our crude material into finished products, must come from the North, unless something is done to educate our people in the industrial arts.

Southern Tradesmen

◆

The Wealth of the South

The opening of the eyes of the world to the vast material wealth of the South will simply mean that strangers will come in and dispossess our own people of their vintage and turn to their own account the opportunities we have never learned to apply.

Board of Trade Meeting (Thomasville, Georgia)

◆

Correct Vision

We should learn to see things in a higher light.

Pittsburgh, Pennsylvania

What Is Taught at Tuskegee

The course of study at Tuskegee corresponds with a high-school course in the North, with foreign languages left out. Special attention is given to the sciences, particularly the science of teaching. It is religious, but not denominational.

In the Black Belt

♦

The Conqueror's Limitations

Neither the conqueror's bullet nor fiat of law could make an ignorant voter an intelligent voter; could make a dependent man an independent man; could give one citizen respect for another, nor a bank account, nor a foot of land, nor an enlightened fireside.

Development of the South

♦

The Higher Law

Men may make laws to hinder and fetter the ballot, but men cannot make laws that will bind or stop the growth of manhood.

Century Club (Indianapolis)

What Ignorance Costs

The Georgia Legislature has before it a bill, recently introduced, proposing to greatly reduce the amount of money annually appropriated for the education of the black youth of that State, on the ground that it cannot afford to spend so much money for Negro education. I would reverse the proposition. I would say, with all the earnestness of my soul, that the State of Georgia is not able to let the 800,000 Negroes within her borders grow up in ignorance. It will cost Georgia more not to educate them than to educate them.

Address at Thomasville, Georgia

◆

Intrinsic Worth

Alongside of the work of wise legislation must go a force that will create a foundation on which we can stand and demand our rights, because of our intrinsic worth to the body politic.

Open Letter to T. Thos. Fortune

The Bread and Meat Side

In spite of all talk of exodus, the Negro's home is permanently in the South; for, coming to the bread and meat side of the question, the white man needs the Negro, and the Negro needs the white.

Madison National Association

◆

Decrease of Crime

Crime among us decreases as ownership in property increases.

Negro Conference

◆

The Pilgrim Fathers

We forgot the industrial education that was given the Pilgrim Fathers of New England in clearing and planting the cold, bleak, and snowy hills and valleys, in the providing of shelter, founding the small mills and factories, in supplying themselves with home-made products, thus laying the foundation of an industrial life that now keeps going a large part of the colleges and missionary effort in the world.

Democracy and Education

Begun by Lincoln

The North should help the South educate the Negro, if it would finish the work begun by Abraham Lincoln.

The Rise of the Negro

Work in the Black Belt

I believe that the majority of students who graduate from Tuskegee should work in what is known as the "Black Belt" of the South, and I am glad that the majority of our graduates have done so thus far, and are working in one way and another for the elevation of those about them. You will hear many students, especially those in the higher classes, say that they intend to practice medicine, study law, or something else, when they graduate; but the majority, after all, will be found in these fields of work that lie about in the black belt of the South, where our best talent and influence are needed.

Sunday Evening Tuskegee Talks

Leadership of the Masses

Can you afford to put alongside the advantages and stimulus that the race will derive from your example of leaders in the field of letters, professional life, and as financiers, such considerations as personal inconveniences and the curtailment of political privileges; considerations which exist but for a day, while the good influence that a single one may exert in some department of life at this auspicious time may incite the youth of far-off ages to new life and hope, by rekindling their faith and aspirations?

Negro's Future

◆

A Refined Family

A quiet development of ourselves and the influence of an educated, refined colored family would gradually and insensibly wear off a prejudice that could never be argued away.

Negro Conference

◆

Foresight

A race of people is a success just in proportion ;
race is able to plan today for a hundred years to
Sunday Evening Tuske

Swine-Raising

Swine-raising has almost become a science or profession. Ignorant labor can no more produce the finest Berkshire and Jersey red hogs than ignorant labor can operate the finest machinery.

Industrial Education in the South

The New Plough

One man in the West, riding behind two fine horses, sitting upon a machine that laps off two furrows at a time, and drops and covers the corn at the same time, does as much work as four Southern corn-planters of the present method of planting corn. So long as this is true, so long will the South buy corn from the West.

Annual Tradesmen

Sound Mind and Body

A person cannot succeed in anything without a good, sound body—a body that is able to stand up against hardships, that is able to endure. A great many of our young men and women, especially in the larger cities, undermine their constitutions, and to a large extent throw away their usefulness, because they do not understand how to take care of their bodies. Do not keep late hours. Have a time to go to bed, and have enough self-control to say to those who would persuade you to dissipate, "My time for rest has come, and you must excuse me."

Sunday Evening Tuskegee Talks

Where Resistance Begins

As long as the Negro will be about the streets drunk, lazy, and shiftless, there is no resistance to him. The resistance comes when he begins to move forward.

The Negro's Way to Liberty

The Great Problem

The great problem is, how to get the masses to the point where they can be sure of a comfortable living, and be prepared to save a little something each year. This can be accomplished only by putting among the masses, as fast as possible, strong, well-trained leaders in the industrial walks of life.

Public Opinion

Most Competent Workman

The man most competent to render efficient service is that man who comprehends most completely the mental as well as the physical phase of labor, and he is most competent as a workman whose mental development has had the most attention.

Greater Opportunities

The Higher Education

The colored boy has been taken from the farm and taught astronomy—how to locate Jupiter and Mars—learned to measure Venus, taught about everything except that which he depends upon for daily bread.

Why Push Industrial Education in the South?

Misdirected Effort

It seems to me that the temptation in education and missionary effort is to do for people that which was done a thousand years ago, or is being done for people a thousand miles away, without always making a careful study of the needs and conditions of the people whom we are trying to help. The temptation is to run all the people through a certain educational mould, regardless of the condition of the subject or the end to be accomplished.

Democracy and Education

◆

His Inheritance

The prime condition of slavery was to keep closed every avenue to knowledge. The Negro had no estate, no family life. His sole inheritance was his body.

The Negro's Way to Liberty

◆

Art and Music in Log-Cabins

Art and music to people who live in rented houses and with no bank account are not the most important subjects to which attention can be given. Such education creates wants without a corresponding ability to supply these increased wants.

Christian Work

The Saddest Sight

One of the saddest sights I ever saw in the South was a colored girl, recently returned from college, sitting in a rented one-room log-cabin attempting day by day to extract some music from a second-hand piano, when all about her indicated want of thrift and cleanliness.

Increased Wants

◆

How to Unite High and Low

It seems to me that one of the most vital questions that touches our American life is how to bring the strong, the wealthy, and learned into helpful touch with the poorest, most ignorant, and humble, and at the same time make the one appreciate the vitalizing, the strengthening influences of the other.

Alumni Dinner (Harvard University)

◆

Poverty and Ignorance

Among the masses there is a great amount of poverty and ignorance, and much need of moral and religious training.

Touching the Masses

The White Neighbor

If the colored woman would make a more attractive home than her white neighbor, that white woman would in time at least be hanging on her gate to make inquiries; and if the colored man knew how to raise forty bushels of corn where the white man could only raise twenty, he would soon be inside the gate to find out the method.

Negro Conference

◆

A Contrast

Is there not as much mental discipline in having a student think out and put on paper a plan for a modern dairy building as having him merely commit to memory poetry that somebody else thought out years ago?

Christian Work

◆

Disposing of the Negro

It has been said that the whites will absorb the blacks, and thus settle the "Negro Problem." Still another proposition is to put the colored people in a part of the country entirely by themselves. This would require the building of a wall to keep the blacks in, and another wall to keep the whites out. The only way to settle the question is to treat the Negro as you would treat any other man; treat him as a brother and a citizen, and there will be no further talk about the much vexed "Negro Problem."

The Rise of the Negro

◆

Sound Advice

We must keep out of debt, avoid lawsuits, and treat our women better.

Negro Conference

◆

How to Fight Prejudice

The most effective ammunition with which to fight prejudice is men who, in every act and thought, give the lie to the assertion of his enemies, North and South, that the Negro is inferior to the white man.

The South as an Opening for a Career

The Great American Heart

My part is to help speed the day, now fast approaching, when there shall not be a Northern heart and a Southern heart, a black heart and a white heart, but all shall be melted by deeds of sympathy, patience, and forbearance into one heart—the great American heart—whose highest aspirations shall be to give to all men everywhere unrestricted opportunity for the fullest growth and prosperity.

Hamilton Club (Chicago)

"A Condition, Not a Theory"

The black man who spends ten thousand a year in freight charges can select his own seat in a railroad train, else a Pullman palace car will be put on for him.

Race Progress

The Conscientious Worker

You will gain a great deal if you will resolve that in all work you perform, whether sweeping a floor, laying off a furrow, building a house, drawing a plan, or studying a lesson, you are going to be perfectly conscientious. If you choose those three lines on which to rest your lives—truthfulness, honesty, and conscientious performance of duty—your future success is assured.

Sunday Evening Tuskegee Talks

◆

Gains Against Losses

Though the line of progress may seem at times to waver, now advancing, now retreating, now on the mountains, now in the valley, now in the sunshine, now in the shadow, the aim has ever been forward, and we have gained more than we have lost. If today we have fewer political conventions, we have more economic gatherings. If we have fewer political clubs, we have more building and loan associations. If we cherish fewer air-castles, we own more acres of land and more homes than has ever been true in the history of the Negro race. If we have fewer men in Congress, we have more merchants and more leaders in commerce.

Hampton Institute Anniversary, '98

Christian Heathen

Many of our people without knowing it are Christian heathen, and demand as much missionary effort as the heathen of foreign fields.

New England Woman's Club

Basis of Success

There are a few things that we must recognize in the beginning if we would succeed, and if we do not recognize that we must have certain qualities and elements in us, we cannot succeed. We cannot succeed unless we recognize that we must have a certain amount of ground work and foundation, and without good foundation we shall find all our efforts largely in vain.

Sunday Evening Tuskegee Talks

A Century's Meaning

One hundred years in the life of a state means much. One hundred years in the life of any church means more. One hundred years in the life of a religious body born in poverty, in the midnight of bondage, amidst the throes and groans of slavery, surrounded and penetrated by oppression and lack of opportunity, furnishes an occasion for supreme thanksgiving and congratulations. Then thirty dollars in property, now three million five hundred thousand dollars; then twenty in church-membership, now five hundred thousand; then one minister of the Gospel, now four thousand, besides nine bishops; but the record is not complete. Blot out this property and these numbers, and the church with such a birth, that could within a century produce a Price, a Dancy, a Hood, or a Walters, and set the world an example in its ability for self-dependence and self-government, would have, with these achievements alone, more than justified its existence.

Centennial A.M.E. Zion Church

Specialization

Learn all you can, but learn to do something, or your learning will be useless.

Sunday Evening Tuskegee Talks

What Makes Social Mudsills

The Negro, no less than his Caucasian brother, must predicate his future wealth, progress, and power upon the industrial system which will secure to him a respectable place in the skilled trades and avocations, or he will in the future have to live upon wages which will be exceedingly meagre, and at last find himself face to face with conditions which will push him to the wall.

Industrial Basis

◆

Self-Confidence

The fact that a man goes into the world conscious that he has within himself the power to create a wagon or a house gives him a certain moral backbone and independence in the world that he could not possess without it.

Century Club (Indianapolis)

◆

Help Ignorant Ministers

Because a minister is ignorant or immoral, I don't believe you gain anything by attempting to get rid of him. I don't believe you gain anything by that kind of procedure. You gain more by helping him get rid of his faults, trying to help him become more intelligent; and in that way, instead of having to spend your force in fighting somebody, you spend it in making a friend that is going to be of some value to you and the people in the community. This is the method which many foreign missionaries are adopting. Instead of their going to Africa, China, and other heathen countries fighting the religious customs of the natives, they are going to take hold of their religion and get out of it whatever is good upon which they can build a stronger and better religion.

Sunday Evening Tuskegee Talks

New Wine in Old Bottles

Not much religion can exist in a one-room log-cabin or on an empty stomach.

Progress of the Negro

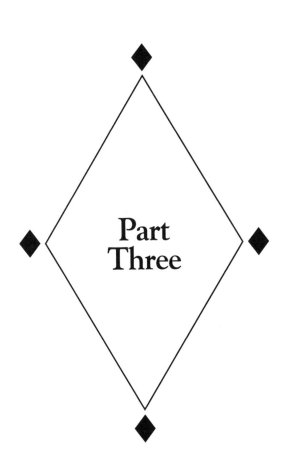

Part
Three

The False and the True

The progress along material lines is marked, yet the greatest lesson that we have learned during the last two decades is that the race must begin at the bottom, not at the top, that its foundation must be in truth and not in pretense. We have learned that our salvation does not lie in the direction of mere political agitation or in hating the Southern white man, but that we are to find a safe and permanent place in American life by first emphasizing the cardinal virtues of home, industry, education, and peace with our next-door neighbor, whether he is white or black.

Hampton Institute Anniversary, '98

Faithful in Small Things

If you are at the head of a stable or barn, plan day by day how best to provide for your horses and cows. When you make yourself master of these humble positions, you will find that the higher calls will soon come to you.

Sunday Evening Tuskegee Talks

Works for Dishonesty

I claim that any training that increases the wants of the individual, especially as that training is applied to a people whose condition is that of the masses of the South, any education that increases wants without increasing abilities to supply these increased wants, is a mistake; and whenever it is done, whether among black people or among white people, you will find unhappiness, unrest, or, too often, dishonesty.

Our New Citizen

Never Wore Neckties

There are a million and a half black men in the South who have never worn a necktie, but send them to school and educate them and they will want neckties, cuffs, and, instead of the bare floors in their little log-cabins, they will want carpet in neat frame houses.

Negroes and Mortgages

Relations with General Armstrong

I account it one of the privileges of my life that for ten or twelve years I have had the opportunity of being closely and intimately connected with such a character [as General Armstrong]; and in being connected with that man, one was always sure that he was being touched by the best and highest type of Christian manhood in any country.

Sunday Evening Tuskegee Talks

◆

Bad Associations

Some of the ways in which young men and women are likely to go astray, especially when they go off to school, is in yielding to the temptation to spend their time with persons who have mean and low dispositions, persons with whom you would be ashamed to have your parents know that you kept company. Avoid that. Be sure that the young man or woman with whom you associate is a person who is able to raise you up, make you stronger in every way.

Sunday Evening Tuskegee Talks

◆

The Curse of the Race

Sentimental Christianity, which banks everything in the future and nothing in the present, is the curse of the race.

Education

"Higher Criticism"

Colored people are not much on your "higher criticism" down South, but they believe in hell—real hell-fire; and if you once make a colored man believe that he will be punished hereafter for drinking whiskey, he will never touch another drop. Moreover, the Negro believes what he reads, and takes the most that he can see in print for gospel truth. Put temperance tracts and primers into the hands of colored people and you will soon see temperance spread all over the South.

The Negro's Beliefs

◆

Expecting too Much

You cannot expect a race to renounce at once the teaching of centuries, without guidance and leadership.

Progress of the Negro

◆

Healing Power

Now, if all our graduates, wherever they go, carry with them this healing power, this power that will cure merely by letting people come in contact with them, even in the slightest manner, if they catch something of the Christ-like spirit, we can have a heaven, as it were, on earth. I do not believe in waiting for heaven to take place in the hereafter. If we imitate the life of Christ as nearly as possible, heaven will come about more and more here on earth.

Sunday Evening Tuskegee Talks

♦

Easy to Be a Hero

On the battlefield, when surrounded and cheered by pomp, excitement, and admiration of devoted comrades, and inspired by strains of martial music and the hope of future reward, it is comparatively easy to be a hero, to do heroic deeds.

Heroes in Common Life

♦

Slavery Degraded Labor

There are several reasons why the South should give special attention to the matter of industrial education. Slavery taught both the white man and the Negro to dread labor—to look upon it as something to be escaped, something fit only for poor people and slaves.

Industrial Education in the South

Non-Essentials

To hold our own, we have no time to spend fretting over non-essentials.

Industrial Education

The Head Cook

Not long since, when in Chicago, I noticed in one of the fashionable restaurants a well-dressed, fine-looking man, who seemed to be the proprietor. I asked who he was, and was told that he was the "chef," as he is called—the head cook. Of course, I was astonished to see a man dressed in such a stylish manner, and presenting such an air of culture, filling the position of chief cook in a restaurant, but I remembered then, more forcibly than ever, that cooking had been transformed into a profession, into dignified labor.

Sunday Evening Tuskegee Talks

What the Negro May Own

There is a custom that prevents a black man in some parts of our country from sleeping in a hotel, or eating in a restaurant, or riding in a first-class car. The average black man has the opportunity only to be denied this privilege about twice a year; but, thank God! there is no law or custom that prevents him from occupying the most convenient, comfortable, and attractive residence, and sleeping in the most luxurious bed, and dining at the best table in the country for three hundred and sixty-five days in the year.

Prejudice and the Negro

Reciprocity

Two nations or races are good friends in proportion as the one has something by way of trade that the other wants.

Taking Advantage of our Disadvantages

Time the Sovereign Healer

That which was three hundred years being woven into the warp and woof of our democratic institutions could not be effaced by a single battle, magnificent as was that battle; that which for centuries had bound master and slave, yea, North and South, to a body of death, could not be blotted out by four years of war, could not be atoned for by shot and sword, nor blood and tears.

Shaw Monument Unveiling (Boston)

Must Be Retrained

The black man must be given the training necessary to offset the influence of slavery.

Our New Citizen

◆

What Will the Student Do?

The question that should come to each one of you with a force that no other question does, is: "Are you going to act in a way to deserve the interest your parents have for you? How are you going to deport yourself? Are you going to disappoint your parents, or are you going to fulfill their highest expectations? Are you going to fill their hearts with sorrow and disappointment or with joy and gladness, make them feel that their lives are worth living, because of the life you are trying to live?"

Sunday Evening Tuskegee Talks

◆

Church-Membership

Belonging to the church does not, in many cases, mean all that is implied, and is no reason why the bulk of our people are not just as much in need of Christian teaching as any people to be found in Africa or Japan.

Congregational Club

Peculiar Religious Notions

My people have peculiar notions about religion. An old brother came into meeting one night and said: "I have had a bad time since I was here a week ago. I have been sometimes up and sometimes down, I have gnawed hard bones and swallowed bitter pills, and I believe I have broken all the Commandments; but, thank the Lord, I haven't yet lost my religion."

The Rise of the Negro

Improved Material Condition

The material condition of the colored man must be improved before he can be elevated to a sense of his responsibilities as an individual.

Development of the Negro

Religion and Worldly Substance

We might as well settle down to the uncompromising fact that our people will grow in proportion as we teach them that the way to have the most of Jesus and in a permanent form is to mix with their religion some land, cotton, and corn, a house with two or three rooms, and a little bank account. With these interwoven with our religion, there will be a foundation for growth upon which we can build for all time.

Foundation and Growth

A Useful Citizen

A person must be able to earn his living before he can be of much benefit to himself and the community in which he lives.

Sunday Evening Tuskegee Talks

Lessons from a Centennial

The lessons to be gleaned from an occasion like this are so many and varied that one hardly knows where to begin or where to end—lessons of congratulation for what has been, lessons of sober, earnest thought for what is, lessons of hope and courage for what is to be.

Centennial of the A.M.E. Zion Church in New York

Common-Sense Ideas

If you wish to help the South, help educate strong, unselfish leaders, well grounded in industry and religion, and in common-sense ideas of life.

Educational Meeting (Manchester, New Hampshire)

Self-Respect in Ownership

A man never begins to have self-respect until he owns a home. If he owns his house he will see that it does not fall to pieces, and that the fences are kept up.

Sunday Evening Tuskegee Talks

Preparing to Die

The trouble with us is that we are always preparing to die. You meet a white man early Monday morning and ask him what he is preparing to do, and he will tell you that he is preparing to start business. You ask a colored man at the same time, and he will tell you he is preparing to die.

Talks to Tuskegee Townspeople

Strength and Weakness

Individually the Negro is strong, organically he is weak.
                                    Industrial Education

◆

What Tuskegee Students Learn

Have you grown to the point where you can unflinch-
ingly stand up for the right, for that which is honorable, honest, truthful, whether is makes you popular
or unpopular? Have you grown to the point where
absolutely and unreservedly you make truth and
honor your standard of thinking and speaking? If you
have reached this point in your moral development,
you have reached the highest point for which
Tuskegee was founded, for which you come here.
                              Sunday Evening Tuskegee Talks

◆

Lack of Preparation

Unused to self-government, unused to the responsi-
bility of controlling our own earnings, our expendi-
tures, or even our own children, it could not be
expected that we should be able to take care of ourselves in all respects for several generations.
                              Century Club (Indianapolis)

What We Never Reach

None of us ever get to the point where we do not have someone to serve, where there is not somebody above us.

Address to Graduating Class

◆

The Honest Foundation

If you get into the habit of putting in hard and conscientious work, doing a little duty well, no matter how insignificant; if you get into the habit of doing well whatever falls to your hands, whether in the light or in the dark—you will find that you are going to lay a foundation for success.

Elements of Success in Life

◆

"The Faithful Servant"

How vexing and discouraging it is to a man to be compelled every morning to say to A or B, "Do this at nine o'clock, that at twelve, and the other at five o'clock," but how helpful it is to have a person with whom you come in contact anticipate the needs of a certain position of his employer.

Sunday Evening Tuskegee Talks

From Slavery to Freedom

When we consider what it meant to have four millions of people slaves today and freemen tomorrow, the wonder is that the race has not suffered more physically than it has.

Physical Condition of the Negro

◆

Home Influence

I think there is no more serious or important time in a young person's life than when he leaves home for the first time to enter school, or any line of business, and I think I can judge pretty accurately what a person is going to amount to by the way he acts during the first one or two years that he is absent from home. You will find, usually, that if a young man or woman is able to stand up against temptations, is able to practice the lessons that his father and mother have taught him, during the first one or two years that he is away from their guidance and instruction, as a rule, that person will hold up well, will not only keep what his father and mother have taught him, but will add to it the strength and instruction he has gotten from them, and will gain help and inspiration as he goes on, and instead of falling by the wayside, will prove himself a valuable and useful citizen, not only able to help his parents, but the community in which he lives.

Sunday Evening Tuskegee Talks

What the Negro Can Have

There is a custom that sometimes prevents a black man from having the privilege of being invited once or twice a year to sit on a jury in a hot, ill-ventilated court-room; but there is no custom, thank God! that prevents him from having the best strawberry farm, the best Jersey cow dairy, or producing the best milk or butter to be had in his county.

Prejudice and the Negro

Negro Laborer Trustworthy

As compared with Italian and Irish labor, the Negro is far more teachable and trustworthy.

Industrial Education in the South

The Christ-Like Workers

Let no generation of Negroes ever prove ungrateful to those Christ-like workers, the band of noble and heroic Northern men and women who have devoted the best years of their lives to the building up of our schools and colleges in the South, and at a time when to have engaged in such work meant for them complete social ostracism and risk of life, but rather let us

build with our earnest and unselfish deeds monu-
ments to their memories that shall tell succeeding
generations from whence we started.

Sunday Evening Tuskegee Talks

General Armstrong's Personality

To a race just emerging from slavery, with all of its
demoralizing entanglements, the pure, unselfish life,
the emphatic personality of General Armstrong, was
an object lesson in the highest form of human living.

Memorial to General Armstrong

"The Wages of Sin"

If we would live happily, live honored and useful lives,
modeled after our perfect leader, Christ, we must con-
form to law, learn that there is no possible escape from
punishment that follows the breaking of law.

Sowing and Reaping

Their Moses

Seven millions of my people saw that they had in
General Armstrong a savior, a Moses, under whose
leadership there could be no back steps.

Memorial to General Armstrong

The Most Patient Race

To right his wrongs, the Russian appeals to dynamite, Americans to rebellion, the Irish to agitation, the Indian to his tomahawk; but the Negro, the most patient, the most unresentful and law-abiding, depends for the righting of his wrongs upon his songs, his midnight prayers, and his inherent faith in the justice of his cause.

Century Club (Indianapolis)

♦

"Lincoln, the Emancipator"

I would call Lincoln the emancipator of America— the liberator of the white man North, the white man South, the one who in unshackling the chain from the Negro has turned loose the enslaved forces of Nature, and has knit all sections of our country together by the indissoluble bonds of commerce.

The Emancipator

A Message to Harvard

If through me, a humble representative, eight millions of my people might be permitted to send a message to Harvard—Harvard, that offered up on death's altar Shaw and a score of others, that we might have a free and united country—that message would be: "Tell them that the sacrifice was not in vain."

Alumni Dinner (Harvard University)

"Bursting Up"

We are crawling up, working up, yea, bursting up, often through oppression, unjust discrimination, and prejudice; but through them all we are coming up, and with the proper habits, intelligence, and property.

Alumni Dinner (Harvard University)

Upright Character

You may fill your heads with knowledge or skillfully train your hands, but unless it is based upon high, upright character, upon a true heart, it will amount to nothing. You will be no better than the most ignorant.

Sunday Evening Tuskegee Talks

The Negro and the Mule

I don't know how it is, but wherever there are black men there are mules. Indeed, in Alabama, the population consists mostly of black men and mules, in some counties.

Educational Meeting (Detroit)

♦

Civil Rights

Property, brains, and character will settle the question of civil rights.

Development of the Negro

♦

Lack of Purpose

Another element which shows itself in the present stage of the civilization of the Negro is his lack of ability to form a purpose and stick to it through a course of years, if need be, years that involve discouragement as well as encouragement, till the end is accomplished. The same, I think, would be true of any race with the Negro's history.

Industrial Education

A Hard-Working Race

As is true of any race, we have a class about bar-rooms and street corners, but the rank and file of the Negro race works from year to year. Whether the call for labor comes from the cotton-fields of Mississippi, the rice-swamps of the Carolinas, or the sugar-bottoms of Louisiana, the Negro answers that call.

Home Missionary Meeting

In the Black Belt

It is my firm belief that the great masses in the black belts of the South stand most in need, at this time, of that character of education which will lead them along material lines. When they have acquired this, there will come the urgent necessity for the higher training which will fit them for the duties of highest citizenship.

Educational Meeting (St. Paul)

Way to Test a Man's Sincerity

It is not very hard to find a person who will speak good and kind words and be unselfish when preaching a sermon before a great audience; but the way to test the person's real character is to notice his treatment of those who come into daily contact with him, how he speaks to his companions, when his voice is not heard by the public.

Sunday Evening Tuskegee Talks

♦

The Heroic and Grand

Those who think there is no opportunity for them to live grandly, yea, heroically, no matter how lowly their calling, no matter how humble their surroundings, make a common but very serious error.

Heroes in Common Life

♦

Hold Fast to Opportunities

We should not permit our grievances to overshadow our opportunities.

Atlanta Speech

♦

An Honest Ballot

The Negro does not object to an educational or property test, but let the law be so clear that no one clothed with state authority will be tempted to perjure and degrade himself by putting one interpretation on it for the white man and another for the black man.

Constitutional Convention (Louisiana)

Sick and Diseased

We are constantly surrounded by persons who are sick and diseased because of their wickedness, people who are given to yielding to temptation, who are cast down and discouraged in the race of life, unworthy of living because of some unfortunate condition, because of the many mistakes they are making. There are those who want to be made whole again and rid of their ignorance. There are others who want to be helped because of their poverty, because of want and misery. We can very often do much toward healing these persons merely by visiting them and speaking kindly and cheerfully to them. We can cure them very largely of their infirmities by merely giving up something they crave, by merely presenting a bunch of flowers at their sick-room. We can help heal them by sending them an encouraging note or letter, or making inquiry as to their condition. There are thousands of ways in which we can heal persons.

Sunday Evening Tuskegee Talks

A Self-Supporting Race

It is very seldom you see a black hand in any part of this country reached forth for alms.

Our Needs

◆

An Ideal Condition

With the masses of the white people and the colored people in the country and towns well educated, the black man owning stores, operating factories, owning bank stocks, loaning white people money, manufacturing goods that the white man needs, interlacing his business interests with those of the white man, there will be no more lynchings in the South than in the North.

The South and Lynch-Law

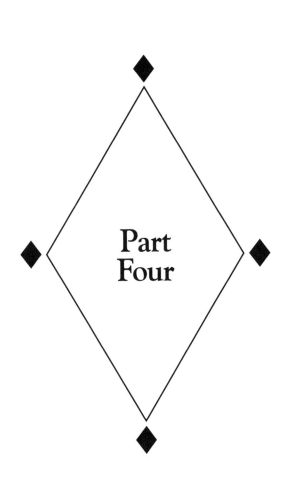

Part
Four

Dying for Others

Three-fourths of the young men and women who are being educated in these Southern schools are being educated at a terrible price; their education being paid for by the lives of such men as General Armstrong, Mr. Hamilton, and other men of that kind, who have been willing to lay down their lives in order that somebody might have a chance.

Sunday Evening Tuskegee Talks

Educated Leaders

If the educated men of the race do not come to the rescue of the masses along industrial lines, the Negro, instead of being the soul and centre of important industries, will be relegated to the ragged edge.

Education

To Conquer Prejudice

Just so sure as the rays of the sun dispel the frosts of winter, so sure will brains, property, and character conquer prejudice.

Armstrong Association

Will not Want for Friends

The black man that has fifty thousand dollars to lend will never want for friends and customers among his white neighbors.

Commercial Freedom

Pippins and Crab-Apples

I would not leave the impression that matters are just right in the South; yet, on the other hand, there is much that is cruelly unjust, unreasonable, much that is hard to bear, and at times, seemingly, dark and discouraging; but I do mean to say that there are more pippins growing in the South than crab-apples and more roses than thorns.

Unitarian Club (Boston)

Which?

The longer I live and the more I study the question, the more I am convinced that it is not so much the problem of what you will do with the Negro, as what the Negro will do with you and your civilization.

Democracy and Education

Higher Education

When I speak of industrial development I do not mean that no attention should be given to what is called higher education. I favor every kind of education.

Lincoln University

♦

He Sticks to His Text

My highest aim is to create the highest possible industrial condition among the colored people of the South. I stick-to this because I believe my people will be better able to cope with the white man and command his respect when they reach a high state of industrial development.

Educational Meeting (Jacksonville, Florida)

♦

Pure and Useful Lives

Make up your mind that in everything, in your thoughts, conversation, and association, it will be your constant endeavor to live in the highest possible atmosphere that can permeate your life, and that your lives will be pure and useful and devoted to the service of your fellow-man.

Sunday Evening Tuskegee Talks

Seen and Unseen

You perhaps noticed, in the chapter which I read, the verse which contains an expression like this: "That the things which are seen are temporal, but the things which are unseen are eternal." Whatever the correct interpretation may be, it seems to me that the hidden things stand for character, and the temporal things are those which stand for reputation. I think the more we think of the matter, of the highest and best things in life, the more readily we will conclude that, after all, it is the hidden things which are most important. It is the hidden things that stand for the highest things in the world. The more important things are those which are hidden; the least important are those which can be seen.

Sunday Evening Tuskegee Talks

Dignity of Labor

No race can prosper until it learns that there is as much dignity in tilling a field as in writing a poem.

Atlanta Speech

No Law Needed

It will be needless to pass a law to compel men to come in contact with a Negro who is educated and has fifty thousand dollars to lend.

Century Club (Indianapolis)

♦

The Mortgage System

The Southern mortgage system is the curse of the Negro. It is the mortgage system which blinds him, robs him of independence, allures him, and winds him deeper and deeper in its meshes each year till he is lost and bewildered.

Unitarian Club (Boston)

♦

Self-Examination

It is a good practice for a person to get in the habit of making an examination of himself day by day, to see to what extent his thoughts have dwelt on those things which are high, and to what extent he has permitted himself to yield to the temptation of being low, in his thoughts and imaginings.

Sunday Evening Tuskegee Talks

Superficial and Ornamental

We shall prosper in proportion as we draw the line between the superficial and the substantial, the ornamental in life and the useful.

Armstrong Association (New York)

◆

Ill-Will and Hatred

No race can cherish ill-will and hatred toward another race without its losing in all those elements that tend to create and perpetuate a strong and healthy manhood.

Our New Citizen

◆

How to Use Education

The great problem confronting us, as a race, is, what to do with the education we have in our heads.

Charles Street A.M.E. Church (Boston)

Obedience

There is no better test by which you can judge of a person's culture, civilization, or whatever else you may call it, so quickly and so accurately as the way in which that person respects authority and obeys orders.

Sunday Evening Tuskegee Talks

Domestic Economy

It is little trouble to find girls who can locate Pekin or the Desert of Sahara on an artificial globe, but seldom can you find one who can locate on an actual dinner table the proper place for a carving knife and fork or the meat and vegetables.

White Rose Mission (New York)

Neglecting Opportunity

The average man usually has the idea that if he were just somewhere else, in another state or city, or in contact with another race, he would succeed, forgetting too often to utilize the forces that are about him and in hand.

Metropolitan Church (Washington, D.C.)

Mother Earth

I would put as a condition for success in life, whether it relate to the individual or the race, ownership in the soil, cleaving to Mother Earth.

The South as an Opening for a Career

◆

Don't Be Too Modest

Never get to the point where you will be ashamed to ask anybody for information. The ignorant man will always be ignorant if he fears that by asking another for information he will display ignorance. Better once display your ignorance of a certain subject than always know nothing of it.

Sunday Evening Tuskegee Talks

◆

Afraid of Riches

I find that our people are too afraid that they are going to get rich. We read in the Bible that it is as impossible for a rich man to enter Heaven as it is for a camel to pass through the eye of a needle; but don't get afraid, accumulate all you can, save all you can.

Talks to Tuskegee Townspeople

Civil Rights Bills

The best thing to do in regard to civil rights bills is to let them alone, and throw our force to making a business man of the Negro.

Development of the Negro

◆

Magnifying Evil Doing

The Negro that steals a pig or is sent to the chain gang for fighting is usually heard of next day in the daily press; but not always so with the Negro who buys a farm or builds a new house.

Negro's Advancement

◆

Starting from the Bottom

Starting thirty years ago without a foot of land, without a hoe, without a horse, and unused to self-guidance and habits of economy, his mind befogged with ignorance and superstition, could you expect him to have travelled very far in the direction of intelligence, wealth, and independence?

New England Woman's Club

"A Man for a' That"

The Negro needs help in making the white people in the South know and respect him as a man.

Negro as a Man

Demagogues and Despots

The rights of the Negroes in the South are too closely bound up with those of their white fellow-citizens to be sacrificed at the dictation of demagogues and political despots.

South Carolina and the Negro

Material and Industrial Condition

Coupled with literary and religious training must go a force that will result in the improvement of the material and industrial condition.

Ocean Grove, New Jersey

"The Afro-American"

Some say, "Send the Negro to Africa, the land of his fathers." But the white man is fast getting about as much control of Africa as he has of the South. And such advisers forget, too, in speaking of our "fathers' land," that, while Africa is the land of our mothers, the fathers of about a million and a half of us are to be found in the South among the blue-blooded Anglo-Saxons.

Africa and the Negro

♦

Practical Religion

The Negro needs not only that religion that is going to fill his heart, but that kind which is going to fill his stomach, clothe and shelter his body, and employ his hands.

Negro's Religion

♦

Educate the Mothers

How often has my heart been made to sink as I have gone through the South and into the homes of my people and found women who could converse intelligibly in Grecian history, who had studied geometry, could analyze the most complex sentences, and yet could not analyze the poorly cooked and still more poorly served corn-bread and fat meat that they and their families were eating three times a day.

Development of the Negro

Influence of Association

You have got to get into the habit of loving to associate with those persons whose influence is for good and which will make you better and nobler men and women.

Sunday Evening Tuskegee Talks

What Would Jefferson Davis Think?

Close to the spot where Jefferson Davis took the oath of office, swearing to sustain African slavery, a Negro has erected a three-story drugstore. When people go and see the thousands of dollars invested there, it is not in reason that they should try to drive that man away.

The Negro's Way to Liberty

Instrument and End

The individual is the instrument, national virtue the end.

Shaw Monument Unveiling (Boston)

Have a Purpose in Life

The student who goes to school with no special plan, who has no time to study this or that, who has no regular hour for eating or sleeping—you will find that very soon that student will be left behind. No matter how brilliant or active a mind he has, success can only come by planning work.

Sunday Evening Tuskegee Talks

♦

The Mortgage Evil

The first year our people received their freedom they had nothing on which to live while they grew their cotton crops. Funds for the first crops were supplied by the storekeeper or by former masters. A debt was created, and to secure this indebtedness a lien was given on the cotton crops. In this way there was started in the South the mortgage or crop-lien system—a system that has proved a curse to the black and to the white man ever since it was instituted.

Development of the Negro

Common-Sense View

Short talks on the principles of agriculture are much
more helpful to the pupils than time spent in commit-
ting to memory the mountain peaks of Central Africa.

How to Build a Good School in the South

◆

Condition of Misery

Far too often education has raised the standard of life for
the Negro, and has naturally increased his wants without showing him any way to satisfy these new wants.

Our Needs

◆

The Producer and Consumer

The Negro in this country must become, in a more
potent sense, a producer of wealth as well as a con-
sumer. He must become more of a business man,
must enter all avenues of industry. Even now, in
almost every part of our country, there are industries
that mean our life-blood, as it were, that are fast slipping from under us. From being the head and centre
of these industries, as of yore, we are too fast being
relegated to the ragged edge of some of the most

important. I repeat that we must, as a race, enter business, for we are constantly being required to measure ourselves by the side of the business world, and by this test we rise or fall.

Centennial A.M.E. Zion Church

♦

The Anchorage

There is no defense or security for any of us, except in the highest intelligence and development of all.

Atlanta Speech

♦

Best Results

A life is not worth much of which it cannot be said, when it comes to its close, that it was helpful to humanity. There is a large satisfaction to a person who has a work and is doing that work, no matter whether it is independent work, or in connection with someone else. Whether the world calls that work great or small, be sure that you have a work, and that in some degree you accomplish that work so well, that you will in a measure get out of it some of the happiness, some of the satisfaction, some of the joy that comes to a person who has a work and who has succeeded, at most, in a moderate degree in accomplishing the best results from that work.

Sunday Evening Tuskegee Talks

◆

Science of Scrubbing

I have often thought, especially while travelling from city to city through the North, what a good thing it would be to establish a chair in some strong university for the science of scrubbing—yes, the common, homely art of scrubbing. Seldom do we see clean floors; the art seems to have passed away.

White Rose Mission and Industrial Association (New York)

◆

Equality of Opportunity

Let it be said of all parts of our country that there is no distinction of race or color in opportunity to earn an honest living.

Schoolmasters' Club (Massachusetts)

◆

Iron Law of Progress

There is no power on earth that can permanently stay our progress.

Alumni Dinner (Harvard University)

But They Were so Engaged

I cannot believe that on the eve of the twentieth century, when there is more enlightenment, more generosity, more progress, more self-sacrifice, more love for humanity, than ever existed in any stage of the world's history, that you and your fellow members are engaged in constructing laws that will keep 650,000 of my weak, dependent, and unfortunate race in ignorance, poverty, and crime.

Open Letter to B.R. Tillman of South Carolina

◆

Greater "Parliament of Man"

In helping the Negro along the line indicated by Hampton, and sending men and women out every year into the schoolroom, into the shops, on the farm, into the field of domestic science, Hampton is making men and women who are shaping the laws of the country just as truly as he who sits in Congressional Halls. In this greater "parliament of man," the Negro has his opportunity, and through it he will blaze a way to the exercise of every privilege that belongs to him as an American citizen.

Hampton Institute Anniversary, '98

The Negro Can Afford It

The Negro can afford to be wronged in this country; the white man cannot afford to wrong him.

Schoolmasters' Club (Massachusetts)

Question for Students

You go out among a class of people who are cast down, discouraged by the many infirmities of life—people who are craving for the help you can give them—and the question will present itself to you: "Are you going to so live that when these people come into contact with you, and look into your faces, they will be made stronger and better by that contact?"

Sunday Evening Tuskegee Talks

A Corrupt Ballot

No man can have respect for government and officers of the law when he knows, deep down in his heart, that the exercise of the franchise is tainted with fraud.

Constitutional Convention (Louisiana)

True Freedom

There is a higher and deeper sense in which both races must be free than that represented by a bill of sale.

Shaw Monument Unveiling (Boston)

From Fourteen to Eight Million

I know that, whether we are decreasing or increasing, whether we are growing better or worse, whether we are valuable or valueless, a few years ago fourteen of us were brought into this country and now there are eight million of us.

Democracy and Education

What Ignorance Craves

It is with an ignorant race as it is with a child; it craves at first the superficial, the ornamental, the signs of progress rather than the reality. The ignorant race is tempted to jump at one bound to the position that is has required years of hard struggle for others to reach.

Brooklyn Institute of Arts and Sciences

Special Invitation

The Negro is the only citizen of America that came by special invitation and special provision. The Caucasian came here against the protest of the leading citizens of the country, in 1492.

Armstrong Association Meeting (New York)

The Quality of Sacrifice

A race, like an individual, lifts itself up by lifting others up.

Constitutional Convention (Louisiana)

Spread Sunshine

Get hold of the spirit of helping somebody else. Seek every opportunity to make somebody happier and more comfortable.

Sunday Evening Tuskegee Talks

What the North Can Do

It is not a practical nor a desirable thing for the North to educate all the Negroes in the South, but it is a perfectly possible and practical thing for the North to help the South educate the leaders who will go out and reach the masses and show them how to lift themselves up.

Twentieth Century Club (New York)

◆

"By this Sign We Conquer"

Let us imbibe this truth into every fibre of our nature: industry, application to duty, brings happiness and prosperity.

Sowing and Reaping

◆

The Hand and Its Fingers

In all things that are purely social we can be as separate as the fingers, yet one as the hand in all things essential to mutual progress.

Atlanta Speech

◆

It Can't Be Done

It is hard to teach a man to sleep between two sheets when he has but one.

Channing Memorial (Newport)

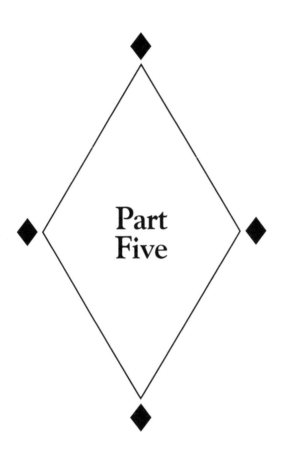

Part
Five

What the Negro Is Doing

It matters not what is said the black man is doing, regardless of entanglements and discouragements, the rank and file of my race is now giving itself to the acquirement of education in a way that it has never done since the dawn of freedom.

Schoolmasters' Club (Massachusetts)

♦

Patience

Our parents, ignorant as they were, taught us patience.

Negro's Advance

♦

A Truth

In business the Negro has a better field in the South than in the North.

Negro Labor

♦

Remedy for Lynching

What is the remedy for lynching? Christian education of the white man and the black man.

Conditions in the South

Commercial Slavery

While bodily slavery is dead, commercial slavery is far from dead.

Progress and the Negro

"The Poor Whites"

So long as the poor whites are ignorant, so long will there be crime against the Negro and civilization.

Home Missionary Meeting (New York)

From Foundation to Turret

Within a quarter of a century the young colored man has been called to learn, and to teach, and to found colleges; not only to learn to read, but to write books, edit newspapers; he has been called to enter commercial life, and to compete with those who have back of them generations of training; he has been called to make laws, and to exercise every virtue and walk in every avenue of life and in the highest civilization the world has ever seen. Were ever young men called to such work before?

The Negro's Way to Liberty

One Standard

In the economy of God there is but one standard by
which an individual can succeed—there is but one for
a race.

Alumni Dinner (Harvard University)

◆

These Should Be Reached

The seriousness of our condition lies in the fact that
in the States where the colored people are most
numerous, eighty-five percent of them are in the
country, and but little is being done for them.

Presbyterian Home Missionary Meeting (New York)

◆

Tuskegee as a Missionary

Tuskegee is sending into numerous communities
model teachers, model farmers, model masons, model
carpenters, model housekeepers. They are able to
transform the locality because they become object
lessons to their own people.

Northfield Conference

Uses of Education

Education itself is worthless. It is only as it is used that it is of value.

Tennessee Centennial

Practice and Teaching

No doubt we might spend hours and days in the recital of the hardships and wrongs of our race, but the question is: How shall we accomplish most good? It seems to me we can do best by seeing how we can deal with the evils we can remedy ourselves. Let us talk simply and to the point, and above all, when we go home, practice what we learn and say.

Negro Conference

True Wisdom

It is a mark of intelligence to be willing to learn even from the most humble person.

Sunday Evening Tuskegee Talks

Cancer at the Heart

The masses of the colored people in the South work, and work hard, but too often their earnings go to pay exorbitant rates of interest on mortgages.

Broadway Tabernacle (New York)

◆

Country Schools

The schools in the country districts in the South rarely last over three months and a half in a year, and are usually held in a church, a wreck of a log cabin, or under a bush arbor.

Sunday Evening Tuskegee Talks

◆

The Great Need

The great need of the Negro today is education.

New York Outlook

◆

Scientific Education

The education that the American Negroes most need for the next fifty or one hundred years should be mostly, but not exclusively, along scientific and industrial lines. When I say scientific, I mean science so applied that it will enable the black boy who comes from a plantation where ten bushels of corn were being raised, to return to the farm and raise fifty bushels on the same acre.

Presbyterian Home Missionary Meeting (New York)

♦

Standing Ground

Standing ground for a race, as for an individual, must be laid in intelligence, industry, thrift, and property.

Shaw Monument Unveiling (Boston)

♦

Knows He Is Down

One of the most encouraging things in connection with the lifting up of the Negro race in this country is the fact that he knows that he is down, and wants to get up—he knows that he is ignorant, and wants to get light.

New York Independent

No Progress Without Friction

You have had an unusual number of accounts of lynching; it seems to indicate a going backward rather than a going forward. It really indicates progress. There can be no progress without friction.

The Negro's Way to Liberty

The Higher Virtues

Says the Great Teacher, "I will draw all men unto me." How? Not by force, not by law, not by superficial glitter. Following in the tracks of the lowly Nazarene, we shall continue to work and wait, till, by the exercise of the higher virtues, by the product of our brains and hands, we make ourselves so important to the American people that we shall compel them to recognize us because of our intrinsic worth.

Century Club (Indianapolis)

Loyalty to Labor

A person cannot render the best service unless he enjoys the work in which he is engaged. You should make an effort to find work in which you will be happy and contented, then be perfectly loyal to that work.

Sunday Evening Tuskegee Talks

Tested by Patience

We are to be tested in our patience, in our forbearance, in our perseverance, in our power to endure wrong, to withstand temptation, to economize, to acquire and use skill; in our ability to succeed in commerce to disregard the superficial for the real, the appearance for the substance. To be great, and yet the servant of all—this, this is the passport to all that is best in the life of our republic, and the Negro must possess it or be debarred.

Alumni Dinner (Harvard University)

Needs Guidance

The Negro has within himself immense power for self-uplifting, but for years it will be necessary to guide and stimulate him.

Awakening of the Negro

Right Will Conquer

Just as sure as right in all ages and among all races has conquered wrong, so sure will the time come, and at no distant day, when the Negro in the South shall be triumphant over the last lingering vestige of prejudice.

Centennial A.M.E. Zion Church

Work for the Ministry

What are some of the problems that the ministry is to help us work out? Our religion must not alone be the concern of the emotions, but must be woven into the warp and woof of our everyday life. Besides, the ministry, the church, must help the educators bring about such a change in the education of the black man that there will be a more vital and practical connection between the Negro's educated brain and his means of earning a living.

Centennial A.M.E. Zion Church

♦

Can the White Man Accept?

I propose in everything that the black man take his place upon the high and undisputed ground of usefulness, honesty, and generosity in all things, and that he invite the white man everywhere to step up and occupy this place with him; and if the white man in all parts of the country cannot accept this invitation, he will thus prove that this is a white man's problem rather than a Negro problem.

Industrial Education

Unreasonable Whims

There should be no unmanly cowering or stooping to satisfy unreasonable whims of Southern white men.

Southern Prejudice

"A Light Set upon a Hill"

Go out and be a centre, a life-giving power, as it were, to a whole community, when an opportunity comes, when you may give life where there is no life, hope where there is no hope, power where there is no power. Begin in a humble simple way, and work to build up institutions that will put people on their feet. It is that kind of life that tells.

Sunday Evening Tuskegee Talks

"Injury to One, Injury to All"

No state in the South can make a law that will provide an opportunity for an ignorant white man to vote and withhold the same opportunity from an ignorant colored man without injuring both.

Constitutional Convention (Louisiana)

Successful and Unsuccessful

Two boys start out in the world at the same time; both have the same amount of education. After twenty years have passed by, we find one wealthy, independent. We find him at the head of a large commercial establishment, employing from one to a hundred men. We find the second boy working for, perhaps, a dollar or a dollar and a half a day, living in a rented house. When we remember that both started out in life equal-handed, we remark that the first boy was fortunate, that fortune smiled on him; that the second was "unfortunate" and "unlucky." There is no such nonsense as that. The first saw how he could put himself in demand, and he kept rising from one position to another until he became independent. The second was an eye-servant who was afraid he would do more than he was paid to do—he was afraid that he would give forty cents' labor for twenty-five cents. He was afraid he would work, perchance, one minute past six o'clock. The first boy did a dollar's worth of work for fifty cents. He was always ready to be at the store before time; and then, when the bell rang to quit work, he would go to his employer and ask was there not something he could do that should be done. Thus the first boy became valuable, and thus he rose higher. We call him "lucky," "fortunate."

Sunday Evening Tuskegee Talks

His Salvation

The salvation of the black man in the South is in his owning the soil he cultivates.

Negro Conference

Engine and Grammar

It requires as much brain power to build a Corliss engine as to write a Greek grammar. I would say to the Negro boy, get all the mental development possible. But I would also say to a large proportion of black boys and girls, and would emphasize it for the next fifty years or longer, that either at the same time that the literary training is being gotten or after it is gotten, they should devote themselves to the mastery of some industry.

Why Push Industrial Education in the South

Light Penetrating

The Southern white people are beginning to see, and the business success of individual colored men is teaching them, that if we turn the colored people loose in the race of life with an equal start with other members of the human family, and the devil is told

to catch the hindermost one, he will not catch a
Negro every time.

Unitarian Association (Saratoga, New York)

Which is the More Costly?

Does ignorance produce more taxable property than
intelligence? Are jails and courts and chain-gangs less
costly than schoolhouses? Is an ignorant citizen more
valuable than an intelligent citizen? Will ignorance
attract more capital to the State than intelligence?

Address (Thomasville, Georgia)

Make No Excuses

If you want to put yourself in demand, make up your
mind that you are going to give as few excuses as possible, and always feel ashamed to give excuses.

Sunday Evening Tuskegee Talks

Treating Him as a Man

He who would succeed with Negro labor must let the
Negro see that he is treated as a man, not as a brute.

Southern States Farm Magazine

The Educated White Man

As the white man in all parts of America becomes more educated, cultured, and more truly a Christian, in that same proportion will the white man be less willing to withhold justice from the Negro.

Future of the Negro Race

Living on Skimmed Milk

Show me a race that is living on the outer edges of the industrial world, or on the skimmed milk of business, and is the football of political parties, and I will show you a race that cannot be what it should be in morals and religion.

Centennial A.M.E. Zion Church

What the World Expects

The world is looking for that man or woman who can tell you why "I can do this or that"—why this was done, how this difficulty was surmounted, and how that obstacle was removed; but the world has little patience with him or her who runs against a snag and gets discouraged, and simply tells why he cannot, and gives excuses instead of results.

Sunday Evening Tuskegee Talks

Universal Brotherhood

I do not attempt to deny the fact that I take a liberal position towards the South, because I believe in the principles of the universal brotherhood of man. If the Southern whites deny this principle, then there is a magnificent opportunity for the Negro to show himself greater than the white man.

Open Letter to T. Thomas Fortune

♦

Chickens from Miscellaneous Sources

Starting thirty years ago with ownership here and there in a few quilts and pumpkins and chickens (gathered from miscellaneous sources), remember the path that has led from these to the invention and production of agricultural instruments, buggies, steam engines, newspapers, books, statuary, carving, painting, the management of drugstores and banks, has not been without thorns and thistles.

Atlanta Speech

This Man Half Free

The white man who would close shop or factory against the black man seeking an opportunity to earn an honest living is but half free.

Shaw Monument Unveiling (Boston)

Passing of the Whitewasher

A few years ago one of the best paying positions that a large number of colored men were doing was that of whitewashing. A few years ago it would not have been hard to see colored men around Philadelphia, Washington, and Boston, carrying whitewash tubs and a long pole into somebody's house to whitewash the walls. They very often not only whitewashed the walls, but the carpets and pictures as well. You go into the North today and you will find a very few colored men whitewashing. White men learned that they could dignify that work, and so began to study the work in schools. They became acquainted with the chemistry composing the various ingredients, learned decorating and frescoing. Now they call themselves House Decorators. Now that's gone to come no more, perhaps. Now that these men have elevated this work and added more intelligent skill to it, do you suppose that any one is going to allow some old man with a pole and bucket to come into his house?

Future of the Negro Race

Bootblacking as an Art

Still another opportunity is going, and we laugh when we mention it. When we think of what we could have done to elevate it in the same way that white persons have elevated it, we realize that after all it was an opportunity; and that was bootblacking. Of course, here in the South we have that to a large extent, because the competition is not quite so sharp as in the North. You go into Montgomery, and want to get your shoes blacked. Very soon you will meet a boy with a box thrown over his shoulders. When he begins to polish your shoes, you will very likely see that he uses a very worn shoe-brush, and unless you watch him very closely, the chances are he will polish your shoes with stove polish. But you go into any Northern city, and you will find that such a boot-black as you meet in Montgomery does not stand any chance of making a living.

Sunday Evening Tuskegee Talks

Lincoln's Pen

With one stroke of the pen the industrial system by which a race of people had been supported for two hundred and fifty years was torn to pieces.

The Emancipator

Wrongs of a Race

Never for a single moment have I been blind to the wrongs perpetuated upon our people, nor have I failed to show my interest in those who call attention to the wrongs; but, while being conscious of the existence of these wrongs, and earnest in my desire to have them righted, I cannot overlook the fact that we have shortcomings of our own which are often made the basis of the wrongs, and which it is not only our duty but to our best interest, from every point of view, to recognize and labor prayerfully to overcome.

Open Letter to T. Thomas Fortune

His Sainted Mother

My first acquaintance with our hero was this: Night after night, before the dawn of day, on an old slave plantation in Virginia, I recall the form of my sainted mother, bending over a bundle of rags that enveloped my body, on a dirt floor, breathing a fervent prayer to Heaven that "Massa Lincoln" might succeed, and that one day she and I might be free.

Twentieth Century Club

The Crucial Test

The crucial test for a race, as for an individual, is its ability to stand upon its own feet and make progress. In demonstrating to the world that the Negro has legislative and executive ability of a high order, this great Christian body has helped the entire race.

Centennial A.M.E. Zion Church

Weakness Changed to Power

Lincoln gave freedom to change sympathies that were local and narrow into love and goodwill to all mankind; freedom to change stagnation into growth, weakness into power.

The Emancipator

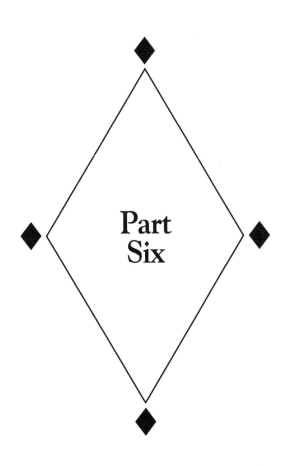

Part
Six

The Pure and the Chaste

Don't get into the habit of using ugly or low language with each other. Young ladies and young men, get into the habit of being satisfied with nothing short of that which is pure and chaste in your conversation; and let others feel when they come into your presence that they must show you respect by being pure in their conversation, and that you love only those things that are high.

Sunday Evening Tuskegee Talks

The Little Green Ballot

There are reports to the effect that in some sections the black man has difficulty in voting and having counted the little white ballot which he has the privilege of depositing about once in two years; but there is a little green ballot that he can vote through the teller's window 313 days in every year, and no one will throw it out or refuse to count it.

Century Club (Indianapolis)

Hunger and Politics

Many of the Negroes in the South are hungry; and when a man is hungry, he cannot get his political rights.

One Solution of the Negro Problem

From Sentiment to Business

The Negro problem in the South is fast passing from a question of sentiment into one of business, into one of commercial and industrial values.

Address (Thomasville, Georgia)

The Fault-Finder

Instead of picking flaws, and making unjust and uncalled-for criticisms on persons and their work, we should contrive to encourage them, that they may improve in it. If there is any good in a thing or a person, let us seek to find the good, and the evil will take care of itself.

Sunday Evening Tuskegee Talks

Indecision

If you have failed thus far to plan out how you are going to spend your time, you are making a mistake and you will find that kind of a mistake largely contributing to your failure in life. Do not go out into the world to hit or miss on some chance, but plan now.

Sunday Evening Tuskegee Talks

◆

Great Need It Is

The great need of the Negro today is intelligent, unselfish leadership in his industrial life.

Schoolmasters' Club (Massachusetts)

◆

Two Tyrants

I know not who is the worse—the ex-slaveholder, who compelled his slaves to work without compensation, or the man who by violence and strikes compels the Negro to refrain from working for compensation.

Democracy and Education

In Freedom's Holy Cause

I cannot forget, as a humble representative of my race, the vacant seat, the empty sleeve, the lives offered up on Southern battlefields that we might have a united country, and that our flag should shelter none but free men.

Our New Citizen

◆

Pre-Eminence of the South

Despite her faults, when it comes to business pure and simple, the South presents an opportunity for business that no other section of the country does.

Negro Conference

◆

Evidence of Growth

You are growing when you get to the point where you can do your best, seen or unseen.

Sunday Evening Tuskegee Talks

Easier of Two Difficulties

The Negro can sooner conquer Southern prejudices in the civil world than learn to compete with the North in the business world.

Dedication Address (Cincinnati, Ohio)

Ham Always on Hand

Wherever there is any business being done, any money to be earned or spent, the son of Ham is found somewhere nearby, and he is going to get some of that money, and is going to spend some.

Mass Meeting (Washington, D.C.)

Idealizing Life

There is a beauty, a transformation, as it were, a regeneration, that takes place in the physical make-up of a young man or young woman who gets into the habit of living on the high side of life rather than on the lower side.

Sunday Evening Tuskegee Talks

The New Emancipation

This is the new emancipation we seek at Tuskegee, to emancipate the white man to love the Negro, to emancipate the Negro into habits of thrift, skill, economy, and substantial character.

Hamilton Club (Brooklyn)

◆

A Self-Evident Truth

I propose that no man shall drag me down by making me hate him. No race can hate another without itself being narrowed and hated.

Carnegie Hall (New York)

◆

His Christian Love

I thank God I have grown to the point where I can sympathize with a white man as much as I can with a black man; where I can sympathize with a Southern white man as much as with a Northern white man.

Hawaiian Gazette

Wisdom of Stupidity

If you are milking cows and feel that you know all that there is to be known about it, you have simply reached the point where you are useless and unfitted for the work.

Sunday Evening Tuskegee Talks

♦

A Two-Edged Sword

With the exception of preaching the Gospel of Christ, there is no work that will contribute more largely to the elevation of the race in the South than a first-class business enterprise. Aside from the direct good to the individual or individuals, a business success cuts as a two-edged sword—bringing from the white man confidence and respect, giving the Negro faith in the fidelity and ability of his own people, and creating at the same time an inspiration that will lead to a higher mental, moral, and material development of the whole race.

Meeting of Directors of Capital Savings Bank
(Washington, D.C.)

Stand Up for the Right

General Armstrong's life purpose was a great lesson—that of showing the world what it means to stand out for a purpose. If you believe a thing is right, the world will honor you all the more for your standing squarely for it.

Sunday Evening Tuskegee Talks

Narrows and Degrades

I claim it narrows and degrades the Negro for him to cherish ill-will for the Southern whites.

Open Letter to T. Thomas Fortune

Angels and Devils in Parties

The sooner the colored man South learns that one political party is not composed altogether of angels, and the other altogether of devils, and that all his enemies do not live in his own town or neighborhood, and all his friends in some other distant section of the country, the sooner will education advantages be enhanced manifold.

Madison National Association

The North's Debt

What of your brother in the South! Those who suffered and are still suffering the consequences of American slavery, for which you and they were responsible—what was the task you asked them to perform? You of the great and prosperous North still owe to your less fortunate Caucasian brethren of the South, not less than to yourselves, a serious and uncompleted duty. Returning to their destitute homes after years of war, to face blasted hopes, devastation, and a shattered industrial system, you asked them to add to their own burden that of preparing in education, politics, and economics, in a few short years, for citizenship, four or five millions of former slaves. That the South, staggering under the burden, made blunders, that in some measure there has been disappointment, no one need be surprised.

Home Missionary Meeting (New York)

◆

"An Eye for an Eye"

No person can give out life without receiving in return life for himself. When we give out the Christlike spirit, something of the healing power, we receive in return strength; and you will find that we shall not only be helping someone else whole, but shall be growing and receiving strength at all times ourselves.

Sunday Evening Tuskegee Talks

How Success Is Achieved

We very often hear it said that the one who has succeeded has been fortunate. It is not so. The fortunate persons, in nine cases out of ten, are those who have had sense enough to lay their plans and bend all their energies toward accomplishing what they have laid out.

Sunday Evening Tuskegee Talks

It Takes Time

You cannot graft a fifteenth-century civilization on to a twentieth-century civilization by the mere performance of mental gymnastics.

Democracy and Education

Doing Right Unseen

It is not very hard to find people who will thoroughly clean a room that is going to be occupied, or to wash a dish that is to be handled by strangers; but it is a hard thing to find a person who will do a thing right when the eye of the world is not likely to rest upon whatever is done. The cleaning of rooms has a great deal to do with forming one's character.

Sunday Evening Tuskegee Talks

Mental Strength the Basis

I would not have the standard of mental development lowered one whit, for with the Negro, as with all races, mental strength is the basis of all progress; but I would have a larger proportion of this mental strength reach the Negro's actual needs through the medium of the hand.

Industrial Training for the Negro

♦

"Barbers" and "Tonsorial Artists"

During the past twenty-five or thirty years we have let some golden opportunities slip from us, and I fear we have not had enough plain talk right on these lines. If you ever have the opportunity to go into the large cities of the North, you will see some striking examples of this kind of thing. I remember the first time I went North—and it hasn't been so many years ago—it was not an uncommon thing to see the barber shops in the hands of colored men. I know colored men who could have gotten comfortably rich. You cannot find today a first-class barber shop in New York or Boston in the hands of a colored man. Something is wrong. That opportunity is gone. Coming home, in Montgomery, Memphis, or New Orleans, you will find that the barber shops are gradually slipping from the hands of the colored men, and they are going back on dark streets and opening little holes. These opportunities have slipped from us largely because we have not learned to dignify labor. The colored man puts a little dirty chair and a pair of razors into a dirtier-looking hole, while the white man opens up his shop in connection with some fashionable hotel, fits it up in fine style with carpets, fine mirrors, etc., and calls that a Tonsorial Parlor. The proprietor sits up at his desk, keeps his books, and takes the cash. Thus he transforms what we call a drudgery into a paying business.

Sunday Evening Tuskegee Talks

Not Easily Forgotten

It is charity and wisdom to keep in mind, in dealing with the two races, the two hundred years of schooling and prejudice against the Negro which the whites are called upon to conquer.

Southern Prejudice

"Know Thyself"

It is an encouraging sign when an individual grows to the point where he can hold himself up for personal analysis and study. It is equally encouraging for a race to be able to study itself—to know its weaknesses as well as its strength. It is not in the highest degree helpful to a race to be continually praised, and thus have its weaknesses overlooked; neither is it the most helpful thing to have its faults alone continually dwelt upon. What is needed is downright, straightforward honesty in both directions.

Development of the Negro

◆

Right to Earn and Spend

The opportunity to earn a dollar in a factory just now is worth more than an opportunity to spend a dollar in an opera house.

Atlanta Speech

◆

Ownership of the Soil

The salvation of the black man in the South is in his owning the soil that he cultivates.

Negro Conference

Difficult Tasks

It is a pretty hard thing to give a man much culture when he has no house to live in; and it is equally hard to make a good Christian of a hungry man.

Public Opinion

◆

Virtue in the Log-Cabin

In that church organization of a hundred members, in the cotton-fields of Alabama, where nine-tenths are in debt for food and clothing, and live from hand to mouth in one-room cabins, there may be much morality and religion, but I had rather take my chances in the community where the minister has taught them to buy land, build comfortable homes and schools, keep out of debt, and to mix with religious zeal plenty of well-cooked, nourishing food, habits of thrift and economy, so that they are able to stand on their feet and look the world in the face, as independent men, in their business and political life.

Centennial A.M.E. Zion Church

Religion

Religion is supposed to be the first business of a church. In proportion to our numbers, intelligence, and wealth, I do not speak irreverently when I say that we have more religion than anything else; and in many sections this seems to be the only article of possession.

Negro and Religion

True Religion

Our people need to be taught that it is better to be a Christian than to be a Methodist or a Baptist; that it is better to save a soul than to subscribe to a creed.

Negro and Religion

Growth of an Idea

Throughout this country we find a system of industrial education entering into all kinds of educational work. If you trace the growth of industrial work, you will find that in nearly every case it owes its existence to the principles so ably defended and started by that grand, unselfish man, General Armstrong, at Hampton Institute, years ago.

Sunday Evening Tuskegee Talks

Not at All Possible

Until there is industrial independence it is hardly possible to have a pure ballot.

Democracy and Education

♦

"Love Thy Neighbor"

The greatest thing you can learn is the lesson of brotherly love, of usefulness, and of charity.

Sunday Evening Tuskegee Talks

♦

Freed the North and South

To the white man who landed at Jamestown, years ago, with hopes as bright and prospects as cheering as had those who stepped ashore on Plymouth Rock, Lincoln, for the first time, gave an opportunity to breathe the air of unfettered freedom.

The South as an Opening for a Career

The Common Highway

There is a highway that shall lead both races out into the pure, beautiful sunshine, where there will be nothing to hide and nothing to explain, where both races can grow strong and true and useful in every fibre of their being.

Constitutional Convention (Louisiana)

◆

Dignifying Labor

The South is beginning to see labor raised up, dignified, and beautified, and in this sees its salvation. In proportion as the love of labor grows the large idle class, which has long been one of the curses of the South, disappears.

Awakening of the Negro

◆

Where the Negro Disappears

When it comes to the production of cotton, the Negro is the main factor; when it comes to the working of the cotton into finer fabrics, where the profit appears, the Negro disappears as a factor.

Public Opinion

Scientific Education

As a race, we should devote ourselves largely to the sciences, because of the practical use we can get out of them, because of the connection we can make with our knowledge of science and our ability to earn a living.

Sunday Evening Tuskegee Talks

◆

The Great Benefactor

Yes, to us all, your race and mine, Lincoln has been a great emancipator.

The Emancipator

◆

Poor Whites of the South

The educators, the statesmen, the philanthropists, have never comprehended their duty toward the millions of poor whites in the South, who were buffeted for two hundred years between slavery and freedom, between civilization and degradation, who were disregarded by both master and slave.

Democracy and Education

◆

Half Free

The black man who cannot let love and sympathy go out to the white man is but half free.

Shaw Monument Unveiling (Boston)

The Negro's Salvation

General Armstrong felt sure that the education of the hand was the surest salvation for the Negro race, and his faith in the practicability of his plan was implicit. And that principle, started by General Armstrong years ago, when it was small, and he was misunderstood and harshly criticized, has gradually worked its way into the whole educational system of not only the South, but of the North and West, for white and black boys and girls alike.

Sunday Evening Tuskegee Talks

What We Shall Do

It is said we shall be hewers of wood and drawers of water, but we shall be more; we shall turn the wood into houses, into machinery, into implements of commerce and civilization; we shall turn the water into electricity, into dairy and agricultural products, into food and raiment.

Our New Citizen (Hamilton Club, Chicago)

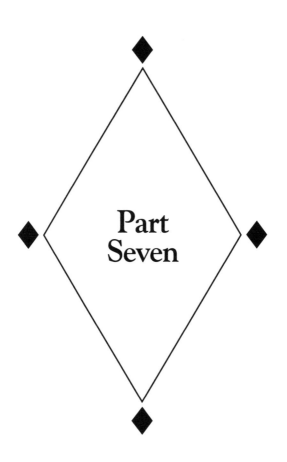

Part
Seven

Physical and Moral Courage

That education, whether of black man or white man, that gives one physical courage to stand in front of a cannon and fails to give him moral courage to stand up in defense of right and justice, is a failure.

Democracy and Education

◆

Which?

Physical death comes to the one Negro lynched in a county, but death of the morals, death of the soul, comes to the thousands responsible for the lynching.

Brooklyn Institute of Arts and Sciences

◆

Hurts Whites More than Blacks

Any law controlling the ballot that is not absolutely fair and just to both races will work more permanent injury to the whites than to the blacks.

Constitutional Convention (Louisiana)

Lowering the Standard

No member of your race in any part of our country can harm the meanest member of mine without the proudest and bluest blood of Massachusetts being degraded. When Mississippi commits crime, New England commits crime, and in so much lowers the standard of our civilization. There is no escape. Man drags man down or lifts man up.

Alumni Dinner (Harvard University)

Easy to Tear Down

It requires little wisdom or statesmanship to repress, to crush out, to retard the hopes and aspirations of a people; but the highest and most profound statesmanship is shown in guiding and stimulating a people so that every fibre in body, mind, and soul shall be made to contribute in the highest degree to the usefulness of the State.

Constitutional Convention (Louisiana)

The Good Part

If others choose to be mean, we can be good; if others push us down, we can help push them up. No harm can come to the black man that does not harm the white man.

Home Missionary Meeting (New York)

◆

"Time and Tide Wait for No Man"

Opportunities never come a second time, nor do they bide our leisure. The years come to us but once, and swiftly pass away, bearing the ineffaceable record we have put upon them. If we make them beautiful years, we must do it moment by moment as they glide before us.

Heroes in Common Life

◆

"You Must Do Something"

As each of you launches out into the world, you must do something; you must labor, you must toil, you must expect to do real hard work, if you expect to reap any reward. In order to get something you must do something.

Sunday Evening Tuskegee ⌐

"Lives of Great Men All Remind Us"

If the Vanderbilts, Girards, Peabodys, and Peter Coopers started out poverty-stricken, with untrained minds, in competition with the shrewd and energetic Yankee, and amassed fortunes, what superior opportunities open up before our young men who begin life with a college-trained mind, and in a locality where competition is at its minimum.

The South as an Opening for a Career

◆

From Dairy to Congress

Suppose you are engaged in milking cows—I think it better to talk of practical things, with which you are acquainted; but I know that many of you boys would much rather have me tell you how you could reach Congress than to prove a successful milker; but I suspect more of us, for a good many years to come, will have to milk cows instead of having a chance to go to Congress, so it won't hurt, I think, to talk just now about milking cows, and if the boy who milks the cow is a success at that, he may lay that as a foundation stone for his future congressional career.

Sunday Evening Tuskegee Talks

Good School-Teachers and Money

Good school-teachers and money to pay them will be more potent in settling the race question than many civil rights bills and investigating committees.

Madison National Association

◆

From One Slavery to Another

The mortgage system, or crop lien law, has almost taken the place of slavery, with all the disadvantages of slavery and few of its advantages.

Our Needs

◆

"We Know Our Rights"

In pointing you to the field, I do not do so as one who believes that the Negro must rise at the expense of the Southern white man, for whatever his wrongs to us he is our neighbor, and the Divine command, "Love thy neighbor as thyself," is broad enough to include him with all his shortcomings; and whenever, by word or act, we can benefit him, let us not withhold our help, but at the same time and under all circumstances show him that "we know our rights, and dare maintain them."

The South as an Opening for a Career

Treasures of Nature

Even the treasures of nature in our South-land, that seem to hide themselves from the hand of man, have felt the inspiring thrill of freedom, and coal and iron and marble have leaped forth, and where once was the overseer's lash, steam and electricity make go the shop, the factory, and the furnace.

The Emancipator

"Excuses Instead of Service"

There is nothing so trying and so discouraging to any man who has the control of any business, or who is responsible for anything, as to be surrounded by a number of persons who are continually giving excuses instead of service.

Sunday Evening Tuskegee Talks

Genius of Success

A teacher who goes into the classroom without having planned her work ahead cannot be a success. The same thing is true in all spheres of life, that a person cannot succeed unless he plans ahead; and the further an individual is able to do this, the more success is going to come to him.

Sunday Evening Tuskegee Talks

Self-Measurement

Now, I want to ask each of you, on this Sabbath evening, to measure yourself in this respect: Take a little more time before you say your prayers tonight and find out if you are growing in your ability to make a living, to love your studies, to control your mind so far as concentration upon your studies is concerned, and in that higher matter of making yourself more useful to the world, and more helpful and cheerful to everyone who touches your life, whether in class or bedroom, whether in the night or day. Are you growing in the matter of making men love you more and of making yourself more useful to every individual?

Sunday Evening Tuskegee Talks

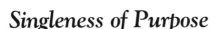

Singleness of Purpose

The only way we can make ourselves useful to humanity and serviceable to God is: (1) by resolving to do something; (2) to do that something, stick to it, improve it, make a specialty of it; and in that way we shall make ourselves useful and reliable.

Sunday Evening Tuskegee Talks

Implements of the Trade

Be sure that you have gotten hold of every book, newspaper, or other publication in which there is something regarding your work; and then don't be content with what you get out of books and newspapers, for that is only the result of somebody else's experience. By conversing with intelligent and experienced persons you can get much valuable information concerning your work.

Sunday Evening Tuskegee Talks

Reaching the Lowest

The science, the art, the literature that fails to reach down and bring the humblest up to the fullest enjoyment of the blessings of our government is weak, no matter how costly the buildings or apparatus used, or how modern the method of instruction employed.

Democracy and Education

World Respects Self-Confidence

Very few people have confidence in a person who is uncertain, constantly vacillating, who does not say directly what he believes; but the world has the greatest amount of respect for a person who believes in a thing and works toward accomplishing that thing in a confident manner.

Sunday Evening Tuskegee Talks

Faulty Education

The study of arithmetic that does not result in making someone more honest and self-reliant is defective. The study of history that does not result in making men conscientious in receiving and counting the ballots of their fellow-men is most faulty. The study of art that does not result in making the strong less willing to oppress the weak, means little.

Trinity Church (Boston)

Child Father to the Man

If the mind is employed during youth as it should be in getting knowledge, in strengthening the faculties, there will follow in manhood and old age a harvest of mental happiness.

Sowing and Reaping

Supreme Unselfishness

Of the many noble traits exhibited by General Armstrong, none made a deeper impression upon me than his supreme unselfishness. I do not believe I ever saw, in all my connection and touch with General Armstrong, anything in his life or actions which indicated that he was in any degree selfish. He was interested in a most unselfish way in the entire work of the South, and anything he could do or say that would benefit another institution seemed to give him as much pleasure as if he had spoken or acted directly for the benefit of Hampton Institute. But for his supreme unselfishness in this respect, Tuskegee could not be anything like what it is today.

Sunday Evening Tuskegee Talks

Influence of Negro Minister

The minister in the Negro church has an influence for good or evil, is looked to for advice on all subjects, to an extent that is not true of any other class of ministers in this country.

Centennial A.M.E. Zion Church

Farms Deserted

We have trained scores of young men in Greek, but few in carpentry or mechanical or architectural drawing. We have trained many in Latin, but almost none as engineers, bridge builders, and machinists. Numbers were taken from the farm and educated, but were educated in everything except agriculture. Hence they had no sympathy with farm life, and did not return to it.

New York Independent

Head and Hand Education

The mere pushing of knowledge into the heads of a people without providing a medium through the hands for its use is not always wise.

The Emancipator

What Institutions Should Teach

Educational institutions all over the South are of little value unless they can pave the way to make results of their work felt among the masses of the people who are especially remote from these institutions.

Sunday Evening Tuskegee Talks

Elements of Power

The man that has the property, the intelligence, the character, is the one that is going to have the largest share in controlling the government, whether he is white or black, whether in the North or in the South.

Century Club (Indianapolis)

Low Wages

How many of our race declare that they won't work for nothing—that wages are low! Isn't it worse to loaf on the street corners than to work for nothing? You get no pay for loafing, do you?

Talks to Tuskegee Townspeople

No Difference

An educated man on the streets with his hands in his pockets is not one whit more benefit to society than an ignorant man on the streets with his hands in his pockets.

Hampton Meeting

Safety in Employment

Something to occupy constantly, during all seasons of the year, the masses of the people in the South, will do as much as any other force to solve the Southern problem.

Christian Work

Sowing and Reaping

If you could look about the South and see the shiftless way in which the people are living, you would think the case almost hopeless. I have felt so. If you could see some of those men, you would realize as never before the awful curse of slavery. You would realize that "Whatsoever a man soweth that shall he also reap."

The Negro's Way to Liberty

More Costly

Ignorance is more costly to any State than education.

Constitutional Convention (Louisiana)

His Place

It is only as the black man produces something that makes the markets of the world dependent upon him for something will he find his rightful place.

The Emancipator

◆

Object Lesson

In addition to making it [Tuskegee] a place where one can behold an object lesson in the best development of the Negro race, in addition to making it an industrial institution, I want to make it a model colony or community for colored people.

Romances in Real Life

◆

Present Conditions

At Tuskegee this is kept uppermost—to train men and women in head and heart and hand to meet conditions that exist right about them, rather than conditions that existed centuries ago, or that exist in communities a thousand miles away.

Presbyterian Home Missionary Meeting (New York)

Hard Cash

Matters of sentiment disappear when placed side by side of the desire for cold, hard cash.

Nashville Centennial

◆

Erroneous

Too often, when the subject of industrial education is mentioned, some get the idea that industrial education is a synonym for limited mental development.

White Rose Mission (New York)

◆

Leap from Slavery to Freedom

Our greatest danger is that in the great leap from slavery to freedom we may overlook the fact that the masses of us are to live by the production of our hands, and fail to keep in mind that we shall prosper in proportion as we learn to dignify and glorify common labor, and put brains and skill into the common occupations of life.

Atlanta Speech

How?

It is natural and praiseworthy for a person to be looking for a higher and better position: no one is to be condemned for that. Now arises the question: How are you going to put yourself in demand for these higher and more important positions?

Sunday Evening Tuskegee Talks

Fitness as the Test

No one should expect, demand, or be given a position by virtue of his color, but because of his fitness to fill it.

The South as an Opening for a Career

The Highest Civilization

To accord the highest justice to the most humble is a sign of the highest civilization. To withhold it is a sign of a want of Christian culture.

Future of the Negro Race

"What Happened?"

A black mother in a Northern State had her boy taught the machinist trade. A job was secured. What happened? Every one of twenty white men threw down their tools and deliberately walked out, swearing they would not give a black man an opportunity to earn an honest living.

Democracy and Education

◆

A National Evil

The epidemic of lynching that has prevailed in the South for some time, and seems to be extending into the West, should convince all that the Southern problem cannot be solved by a mere wave of the hand.

The South and Lynch-Law

◆

Faith in God

Never since the days that we left Africa's shores have we lost faith in you or in God. We are a patient people. There is plenty in this country for us to do. We can afford to work and wait.

Presbyterian Home Missionary Meeting (New York)

"Worth Makes the Man"

We mean to prove our worth not by mere talk, or complaints, or fault-finding, and the rest we leave to you.

The Emancipator

♦

Fruits of His Labors

It is a great thing for a person to accomplish something in this world. I think General Armstrong's greatest satisfaction before he died was that he had a mission which he had seen bear fair fruit. He had a great work and he had the supreme satisfaction of seeing the fruits of that work in the lives of the men and women he trained and scattered all over the country.

Sunday Evening Tuskegee Talks

♦

The Negro's Rights

I claim for the Negro all the rights and privileges enjoyed by any other race, but I also maintain that we must have a foundation on which to rest our claims.

Public Opinion

Why the South is Bound to a Body of Death

Why is it that the South today is bound to a body of death? Five cent cotton is like the man hugging the bear, and can't turn him loose, simply because the farmers of the South are not intelligent enough to raise a diversified crop.

Educational Meeting (Topeka, Kansas)

◆

Social Equality

The wisest among my race understand that the agitation of the question of social equality is the extremest folly, and that progress in the enjoyment of all the privileges that will come to us, must be the result of severe and constant struggle rather than of artificial forcing. No race that has anything to contribute to the markets of the world is long in any degree ostracized.

Atlanta Speech

◆

King Cotton

The Negro and the mule are the only forces so far discovered that can produce cotton.

Board of Directors, Capital Savings Bank
(Washington, D.C.)

Self-Knowledge

We should know our weaknesses as well as our strength if we would attain to the best in our civilization.

Trinity Church (Boston)

◆

Right Thing to Be Done

I have always gone on the plan of finding the right of a thing to be done, then working in that direction until I have accomplished it.

Best Way of Building up a Model School

◆

What Would Mother Say?

There is no better way to test an act than to ask yourself the questions, "What would my mother or father think of this? Would he or she approve of this, or should I be ashamed to let them know that I have been guilty of such a performance?" Ask yourselves such questions day by day. I think you can get a great deal of wisdom out of such questions.

Sunday Evening Tuskegee Talks

Lifting up our Fellows

The only thing worth living for is the lifting up of our fellow men.

Address to Graduating Class of '92

♦

The White South's Needs

The white people of the South know the colored people as servants, cooks, waiters, or as chicken thieves. The trouble is they do not come in contact with the black man in the way to know him in the highest sense.

Unitarian Association (Saratoga)

♦

Industrial Education

Industrial education is meant to take the boy who has been following a mule behind a plough, making corn at the rate of ten bushels per acre, and set him upon a machine under an umbrella behind two fine horses, so that he can make four times as much corn as by the old process, with less labor.

Twentieth Century Club (New York)

Harmony

Harmony between the two races will come in proportion as the black man gets something the white man wants.

Quinn Chapel (Chicago)

◆

Competing with the World

At the end of two hundred and fifty years of enforced labor, the Negro finds himself without warning, and with no preparation, competing with the world for a market for his labor.

Mass Meeting (St. Paul)

◆

Unostentatious Charity

It is the quiet, unseen giving, which never reaches the ear of the world, that makes possible the existence of the best things of the world.

Sunday Evening Tuskegee Talks

The Best Labor

Sooner or later this country is going to realize that it has at its very doors the best labor that the world has seen.

Southern States Farm Magazine

The Negro's Guiding Star

Progress, progress is the law of God, and under Him it is going to be the Negro's guiding star in this country.

Chautauqua Assembly